# Managing Diversity

# Managing Diversity

## Institutions and the Politics of Educational Change

Sandra Leslie Wong

ROWMAN & LITTLEFIELD PUBLISHERS, INC.
*Lanham • Boulder • New York • Oxford*

ROWMAN & LITTLEFIELD PUBLISHERS, INC.

Published in the United States of America
by Rowman & Littlefield Publishers, Inc.
4720 Boston Way, Lanham, Maryland 20706
www.rowmanlittlefield.com

12 Hid's Copse Road, Cumnor Hill, Oxford OX2 9JJ, England

British Library Cataloguing in Publication Information Available

**Library of Congress Cataloging-in-Publication Data**

Wong, Sandra Leslie, 1960–
    Managing diversity : institutions and the politics of
educational change / Sandra Leslie Wong.
        p.   cm.
    Includes bibliographical references and index.
    ISBN 0-8476-9492-5 (alk. paper) — ISBN 0-8476-9493-3 (pbk. : alk. paper)
    1. Multicultural education—United States.   2. Curriculum planning—
United States.   3. Textbooks—United States.   4. Educational change—
United States.   I. Title.
    LC1099.3 .W66   2001
    375'.001—dc21                                              2001041703

Printed in the United States of America

∞ ™ The paper used in this publication meets the minimum requirements of
American National Standard for Information Sciences—Permanence of Paper for
Printed Library Materials, ANSI/NISO Z39.48-1992.

To my parents,
Chester and Lilly Wong

# Contents

# Acknowledgments

I am indebted, first, to all of the people I interviewed through the course of my research. I greatly appreciate their time and their willingness to share with me the perspectives and experiences that made this book possible.

I also owe special thanks to two individuals who offered valuable advice and insight as my work developed. Paul DiMaggio gave exceptionally detailed comments on multiple versions of my dissertation thesis as well as enthusiastic support for my ideas. Although this project began many years ago, I have not forgotten his early impact on its progress and on the kind of feedback I now attempt to give my students. Mary Ann Clawsen was instrumental in encouraging me to expand the dissertation beyond the realm of textbook politics and to pursue a broader understanding of the relationship between politics, institutions, and education. I have benefited from and been enriched by her intellectual and professional guidance as a colleague as well as her emotional support and confidence as a friend.

A dissertation grant from the National Science Foundation facilitated the early stages of my research. A two-year postdoctoral fellowship from the University of Iowa and a subsequent Spencer fellowship from the National Academy of Education enabled me to devote time and thought to further research and writing. I am grateful to these institutions for their interest in this study and to Rowman & Littlefield for its publication.

My thanks to my colleagues in the Department of Sociology at Colorado College for giving me a new start, and to numerous folks who have provided friendship, help, or inspiration along the way: Chandler Davidson, Elizabeth Long, Steven Brint, Charles Lemert, Rob Rosenthal, Karen Heimer, Lingxin Hao, Robin Stryker, Susan and David

Scheibner, Norma Torres, and Homer and Henry DePoe. Finally, I wish to acknowledge my family for their tolerance and patience, and my husband Bob, for critically reading my chapters in spite of their jargon, for trying to humor me when my seriousness prevailed, and for loving me even without tenure. May the second time be our charm.

# 1

# Introduction

Since the Civil Rights movement of the 1960s, racial minorities and women's groups, parents, liberals, and conservatives have taken sides in heated debates over whose knowledge counts in public education. These debates about American culture and identity are provocative, challenging, and ever so timely as the ideal of *e pluribus unum* confronts perhaps its greatest challenge since the late 1800s when urbanization and a growing diversity of immigrants produced both societal and educational transformations.[1] As competing views about pluralism and unity continue to surface in contests over the curricular canon, national standards, and school textbooks, we are reminded time and again of the relationship between social interests and educational content.

During the 1980s, struggles over Western civilization courses and multiculturalism on college campuses, fundamentalist challenges to secular humanism, and protests from the cultural Left against Eurocentric textbooks garnered considerable attention among journalists and academic scholars.[2] Identity politics and reactions to these politics took center stage in what became known as the so-called culture wars and further illuminated the role of school knowledge in legitimating and maintaining particular meanings and beliefs.[3] By the end of the twentieth century, concepts such as diversity and multiculturalism had become a common part of educational discourse, and today it is tempting to conclude that contestations over new ideas have produced fundamental changes in what young people are taught.

What is missing from analyses of cultural conflicts, however, is the sociological question of whether and how the issues that divide parents, communities, politicians, and academic theorists relate to the actual selection of knowledge and the transmission of new ideas. In this book, I argue that even though struggles over knowledge spawn controversy, the institutional decisions that create and maintain the content of "official" school knowledge are usually made independently of such cultural politics. Whether battles over the representation of diversity are couched in the 1960s' language of inclusion or the 1990s' discourse of multiculturalism, the stakes are rarely as high as activists from either side hope or fear they will be. Understanding why this is so requires that we consider not only the battles taking place over educational content—the stuff of cultural politics—but also the mechanisms by which knowledge is chosen, packaged, and taught. These mechanisms include features of educational organization such as contexts of decision making, timetables, procedures, and rules as well as abstract rubrics, frames of reference, and rationales about what is right, feasible, or necessary according to specific notions of the functions of schooling.

This book examines how decisions about school knowledge are made, by whom, and in which decision-making sites. Its primary impetus is to move beyond the philosophical and symbolic arguments of curricular struggles to show how educational decision makers think and how multiple expectations, many of which are not overtly or exclusively ideological, affect their choices and behaviors.

## WHO SHOULD KNOW WHAT: THE CASES OF TEXAS AND NEW YORK

To explain my view of the relationship between cultural politics, official knowledge, and institutional decision making, I focus on struggles over school knowledge in two different periods and two different sites. The first case is a system of textbook adoption in the state of Texas, one of twenty-two states that approves schoolbooks at the state level before offering them for adoption to local school districts.[4] Texas is also the single largest market for secondary-level textbooks in the United States and buys 95 percent of a six-year supply in the first year of a book's adoption. The magnitude of the state's purchase and its lump-sum payment are valuable for successful schoolbook publishers who can recoup some of their production costs almost immediately.[5]

Since the early 1960s, Texas's selection process has also been recognized as a site of public activism. As groups with competing ideas have made their views known, their well-publicized participation and perceived influence has reinforced a common belief that "the political and ideological climate of . . . primarily southern states [such as Texas] often determines the content and form of purchased curriculum throughout the rest of the nation."[6] In particular, from the early 1970s to the mid-1980s, struggles over issues of representation and inclusion drew attention to the state as an important setting in which to assess the impact of new perspectives on textbook content and selection.

By the early 1990s, diversity continued to be a central focus of curriculum reform in several states and local school systems. On the one hand, these more recent attempts to include the histories and contributions of different ethnic groups in American history were similar to the agendas of social movements in previous decades. On the other hand, contemporary curricular struggles posed a more significant challenge to long-standing conceptions of American identity. In response to the increasing diversity of their student populations, some states shifted their reform agendas from the goals of inclusion and representation that characterized earlier movements to promoting tolerance and respect for distinct cultural and sexual identities. To examine the outcomes of these reform efforts, my second case involves two sites of curricular struggle in New York, a state-level plan to refashion the social studies curriculum and a local initiative to recognize diverse sexual identities in New York City's primary schools.

The Texas and New York cases provide a basis for examining both the decision-making processes of a textbook adoption system and the dynamics of curricular formation and implementation more generally. In both sites, progressive movements have sought to introduce new knowledge and to emphasize a multicultural, critical approach to learning. And in both contexts, advocates of progressive educational change have encountered resistance resulting in the culture wars about which so much has been written. My purpose is to describe the conflicts engendered by efforts to recognize diversity; however, I argue that while opposition to the principles and ideals of progressive movements has impeded their realization, it is not, in my view, the primary or only obstacle to reconstructive curricular change. Overt cultural and political struggles, at whichever point they occur (schoolbook selection or curricular reform), intersect with institutional processes and professional interests to shape what is taught in schools. These processes and interests more pointedly influence how knowledge is conceptualized, selected, and packaged, and how reform ideas are defined and put into practice.

The issues at stake in cultural politics and the factors that govern decisions about what is taught reveal that social actors think about school knowledge in fundamentally different ways.[7] Those who testify at state-level public hearings and school board meetings or express their views in newspapers and scholarly publications treat the selection and transmission of knowledge as a process of choosing and affirming particular ideas. For parents and activists, decisions about whose knowledge counts are infused with moral, social, and cultural implications; for scholars and cultural critics, these decisions are also viewed as sources of validation for certain paradigms and worldviews.

In contrast, state officials, classroom teachers, and schoolbook publishers conceptualize school knowledge—its purpose, its givenness, its possibilities—in ways tied to their positions in institutions and organizations that are often quite detached from the political fray. For policy makers, knowledge selection is an administrative task as well as a political challenge; for educators, it is a matter of professional expertise and pragmatic imperatives; and for publishers, it is a means of making profit or incurring losses. The primary concerns of these groups have more to do with bureaucratic procedures, teacher and student abilities, and marketing strategies than with matters that stir lively public debate.

Given that similar organizational priorities may be found in other areas of education, the logic of decision making may come as no surprise. Research on tracking and bilingual education, for example, reveals a divide between those who focus on issues of effective implementation and those who are more concerned about the underlying theoretical assumptions of educational policies and their social implications. Nonetheless, it is crucial to understand the importance of institutional priorities more fully if we are to assess the potential for advancing alternative curricular ideas and for realizing transformative changes in knowledge.

By transformative change, I am referring to a particular version of multicultural education, one that addresses not simply the representation of groups, but more important, the relations between groups and their unequal positions in society. It is the version Cameron McCarthy describes when he argues that "a critical approach to multiculturalism must insist not only on the cultural diversity of school knowledge but on its inherent relationality . . . School knowledge," he observes, "is socially produced, deeply imbued with human interests, and deeply implicated in the unequal social relations outside the school door."[8] Thus, reconstructive school knowledge requires making these social relations, group identities, and shared histories visible.

Theorists of radical progressive change similarly envision schools as potential sites of critical consciousness and emancipation, and teachers and students as active agents of change.[9] Peter McLaren proposes a critical multiculturalism that transforms the "social, cultural, and institutional relations in which meanings are generated."[10] Henry Giroux suggests that schools can engage in the reconstruction of culture and social life by affirming students' identities, enhancing their capacity to bring their everyday experiences to the classroom, and encouraging them to see themselves as producers of knowledge.[11] According to these perspectives, school knowledge and curricula are open to multiple, and sometimes oppositional, meanings.[12]

These visions of educational transformation move us beyond deterministic views of knowledge that posit little hope for meaningful curricular change. Theories of reproduction, for example, have largely assumed that school knowledge reflects and reinforces what Pierre Bourdieu terms the "cultural arbitrary," a system of beliefs that "most fully, though always indirectly, expresses the objective interests (material and symbolic) of the dominant groups or classes."[13] Schools teach students not only the technical and social skills consistent with their future positions as productive workers and consumers in a capitalist economy, but also the values, norms, and dominant constructions of reality that support elite interests. Meanwhile, alternative ideas are filtered through a process of "selective tradition,"[14] and conflicting values and meanings are delegitimized.

If cultural reproduction is effective, there should be little or no space for new cultural icons and multiple viewpoints, let alone subversive ideas, and no means by which long-standing beliefs can be questioned. We would expect school curricula and materials to present a one-sided account of historical events and a homogenous picture of American culture. Yet, by assuming that dominant groups are unhindered in their effort to universalize their cultural beliefs, reproduction theories suggest a mechanistic relationship between knowledge and power as well as a degree of hegemonic success that does not allow for and is, in fact, contradicted by evidence of curricular change.

While official knowledge was once synonymous with Anglo-Saxon, Protestant ideology, the curriculum since the 1960s has become more inclusive of the histories and experiences of multiple groups. As social theorist Steven Seidman has observed, new social movements challenged the dominance of White, European, male, and heterosexual viewpoints.[15] Responding to demands for equal representation, colleges and universities created new programs and courses in African, Asian, Latino, Native American studies, and women's studies.[16] At the same time, high school textbooks devoted more attention to women and minorities in order to convey the message that the United States was "a multiracial, multicultural society."[17] These gains are more in keeping with a system of democratic pluralism and status-group struggle than one of uncontested cultural hegemony. As the state mediates "sociohistorical" struggles among social classes and gendered and racial groups, it must strive to address both capitalist interests and the values of a democratic society.[18]

## THE RECONTEXTUALIZATION OF NEW KNOWLEDGES

Although successful movements for inclusion reveal the limitations of deterministic accounts and suggest the possibilities for educational change, we must nonetheless refrain from assuming that transformative educational visions are being fulfilled. Assessing the promise of such visions requires examining the institutional contexts in which the selection and transmission of knowledge actually take place. If school knowledge is becoming more open to multiple perspectives and experiences, where, and more important, how are these changes occurring? How are new ideas introduced, and what are the obstacles to their realization?

I argue that, contrary to the assumptions of reproduction theories, new curricular ideas do gain currency. However, in contrast to transformative visions, once new ideas are mediated through institutional processes they become integrated into existing frameworks and are disarmed of their transformative punch. As Michael Apple theorizes, the cultural capital declared to be official knowledge "is *compromised* knowledge, knowledge that is filtered through a complicated set of political screens and decisions before it gets to be declared legitimate."[19] Hence, concepts such as multicultural education and diversity certainly have the potential to expand or reconstruct the curriculum, but in the process of becoming official knowledge, educators, textbook publishers, state education departments and local school boards recontextualize these ideas.[20] The participation of these groups in the production and dissemination of knowledge requires that we consider the influence not only of elite interests and public mobilizations, but also of the specific logic, meanings, and practices that make sense and seem purposeful to those involved with educational practice.

By identifying and explaining how multiple interests and agendas, some of which are overtly ideological, some of which are not, affect the production and selection of knowledge, we can begin to understand the gulf that often exists between new curricular ideas and classroom practice. Moreover, we gain a clearer picture of the promise and pitfalls of realizing alternative educational visions. This picture tells us that change, while possible, is modest, that new ideas tend to be modified through particular organizational processes and conceptions of knowledge, and that once institutionalized, we gain the benefit of having these ideas in the curriculum, but run the risk of taking their inclusion for granted and believing that we have accomplished meaningful curricular change while ceasing to question what is actually being taught. In his 1997 publication *We Are All Multiculturalists Now*, sociologist Nathan Glazer (1997) does exactly this.

> I too have drawn a lesson from this story, and from much else that is going on in American education. It is that multiculturalism in education—so strongly denounced by so many powerful voices in American life, by historians, publicists, labor leaders, intellectuals, the occasion for so many major battles in American education during the nineties, and so much at odds with the course of American culture, society, and education at least up until the 1960s—has, in a word, won.[21]

But has it? Will dominant constructions of diversity change how future adults think about different racial, ethnic, and sexual identities? I think not, and I believe we are mistaken to think that anyone has "won."

This book asserts that although diversity, inclusion, and multicultural education may be terms at the heart of public and scholarly debates, we would do well to seriously consider whether and how these ideas become a part of official knowledge. Such an inquiry reveals the persistence of dominant models of cultural pluralism, which, combined with standard modes of presenting knowledge, engender cynicism among teachers, skepticism among critics from the Right and Left, as well as tokenistic efforts from publishers and states to implement diluted versions of multicultural education.

In chapter 2, I look at struggles over diversity in textbook knowledge from the early 1970s to the mid-1980s to provide a sense of the kinds of ideological tensions that emerged between progressive and traditionalist groups in the Texas textbook adoption process. To assess the relationship between textbook activism and the process of selecting textbooks, I then examine the potential impact of protests from parents and interest groups in light of how textbook adoption is organized, and the reactions of educators and publishers to input from these groups. I argue that the regulation of public mobilizations and the effort of decision makers to avoid or moderate ideological conflict severely limit the effect of cultural politics on textbook selection.

Chapter 3 turns to the priorities and perspectives of Texas's state textbook selection committees and schoolbook publishers to explain how they influence what is taught. Based on observations of committee meetings and interviews with former committee members, I show how educators approach the task of selecting knowledge with very different assumptions from those of parents and organized interest groups. While the latter groups focus primarily on issues of cultural representation— the absence of minorities or the biased treatment of women and men— adoption committees choose books according to their pragmatic, stylistic, and pedagogical merits. These criteria reflect selection committees' responsibilities to the state, their identities as professionals, how they conceptualize knowledge, and the conditions under which they make their decisions. These factors distance selection committees from cultural conflicts and impede their participation in reconstructing school knowledge. In turn, educators' preferences influence the behaviors of textbook publishers who, perhaps more than any others, determine what knowledge is made available in most public school classrooms. Striving to please teachers and to meet the publishing industry's "bottom line," publishers also pay more attention to matters of utility and practice than to the substantive ideas and viewpoints at the center of educational debates.

In chapter 4, I shift my focus from the parameters of textbook adoption to processes of curricular planning in New York State and New York City. This chapter discusses how the terms of debates over diversity changed by the 1990s to emphasize not merely the inclusion of different groups in school knowledge, but also a new understanding of American pluralism. It illuminates major points of conflict between those who pushed to recognize diverse cultural and sexual identities, and their opponents who argued that social and psychological agendas were supplanting the traditional aims of schooling—to teach a common culture and transmit basic facts and skills.

I then assess the impact of ideological struggles on actual curricular policies. I argue that controversies over pluralism made a more discernible impact on policy making in both sites than did opposition to textbooks in Texas. The authority of elite scholars carried weight at the state level, while the political clout of parents and communities enhanced the power of public voices at the local level. Although neither group prevented the creation of new curricula, both contributed to the modification of potentially transformative mandates.

Chapter 5 examines the implications of New York's curricular reforms for educational practice. I suggest that no matter what ideals curricular policies promote, their realization depends upon how teachers receive and implement policies. I use data from interviews with teachers of U.S. history in New York City high schools to show how teachers respond to new curricular ideas and how their capacity to include diverse perspectives and experiences in their lessons is hindered by the institutional contexts in which they work, by the external expectations that structure their work, and by their own views and interpretations of the meaning of diversity. These conditions and meanings contribute to teachers' skepticism of, and at times, resistance to new policies, as well as their reluctance to embrace the kinds of reconstructive projects and pedagogies that transformative theorists have assigned to them.

In chapter 6, I argue that new educational ideas may appear to move the curriculum in alternative directions, but to assume that they will necessarily reconstruct school knowledge belies their weak formulation in official policies and their limited influence on educational decision makers and cultural producers. I assess the effects of commodification and technocratic rationality on how knowledge is conceptualized and how new ideas are incorporated into conventional modes of practice, and I discuss ways in which meaningful change might come about.

For those who hope to advance critical pedagogies and multiple knowledges, these outcomes are likely to be disappointing. But they are outcomes that warrant our persistent attention if we are to successfully reduce not only the gap between the substance of cultural politics and educational decision making, but also an equally large divide between educational theory and practice. At all levels of education, understanding what diversity means, what we expect to gain by achieving it, and the barriers to doing so are crucial to meaningful change. Despite honorable intentions, curricular expansion will merely be or seem tokenistic without this level of understanding. Examining how we think about social differences and contesting the dominant logic with which school knowledge is created and disseminated remain significant challenges; nonetheless, they are challenges well worth facing if we are counting on schools to enhance the nation's capacity to learn from its diversity.

## NOTES

1. Since Congress changed immigration laws in favor of family reunification with the passage of the 1965 Immigration Act, as many as one million newcomers have arrived in America each year, settling mostly in the nation's largest cities. What is distinctive about recent immigrants is that most come not from European countries, as in the past, but from Latin America and Asia. According to William Booth, while "whites currently account for 74 percent of the population . . . by the year 2050, demographers predict, Hispanics will account for 25 percent of the population, blacks 14 percent, Asians 8 percent, with whites hovering somewhere around

53 percent." In several states, non-Hispanic whites will no longer be a majority. See William Booth, "Diversity and Division," *Washington Post Weekly*, March 2, 1998, vol. 15, 6–7, national edition.

2. See James Davison Hunter, *Culture Wars* (New York: Basic, 1991) for a discussion of battles on multiple fronts.

3. See Todd Gitlin, *The Twilight of Common Dreams: Why America Is Wracked by Culture Wars* (New York: Metropolitan, 1995).

4. The adoption states are Alabama, Arizona, Arkansas, California, Florida, Georgia, Idaho, Indiana, Kentucky, Louisiana, Mississippi, New Mexico, Nevada, North Carolina, Oklahoma, Oregon, South Carolina, Texas, Tennessee, Utah, Virginia, and West Virginia.

5. Arnie Weissman, "Building the Tower of Babel," *Texas Outlook* (Winter 1981–82): 29.

6. Michael W. Apple, "The Culture and Commerce of the Textbook," *Journal of Curriculum Studies* 17 (1985): 156.

7. While battles over school knowledge are fought over many topics and subject areas, my analysis of textbook and curricular struggles focuses primarily on subjects such as American history and civics in which topics related to pluralism and diversity are taught. Though diversity can be and is represented in a variety of subjects, in social studies issues of tone, perspective, and viewpoint are especially important. Hence, although I use the term "school knowledge," frequently throughout the book, I do not mean to imply that the findings of this research are applicable to struggles over all subjects and forms of school knowledge. In fact, different issues will be at stake in other sites of struggle.

8. Cameron McCarthy, "After the Canon: Knowledge and Ideological Representation in the Multicultural Discourse on Curriculum Reform," in *Race, Identity, and Representation in Education* (New York: Routledge, 1993), 295.

9. Stanley Aronowitz and Henry A. Giroux, *Education Still Under Siege*, 2d. ed. (Westport, Conn.: Bergin & Garvey, 1993).

10. Peter McLaren, "White Terror and Oppositional Agency: Towards a Critical Multiculturalism," in *Multicultural Education, Critical Pedagogy, and the Politics of Difference*, ed. Christine E. Sleeter and Peter L. McLaren (Albany, N.Y.: SUNY Press, 1995), 42.

11. Henry A. Giroux, "Schooling As Cultural Politics: Toward a Pedagogy of and for Difference," in *Critical Pedagogy, the State, and Cultural Struggle*, ed. Henry A. Giroux and Peter McLaren (Albany, N.Y.: SUNY Press, 1989), 148.

12. Also see James A. Banks, *Educating Citizens in a Multicultural Society* (New York: Teachers College Press, 1997), 119. According to Banks, transformative academic knowledge "consists of paradigms, themes, and explanations that challenge mainstream academic knowledge and that expand the historical and literary canon."

13. Pierre Bourdieu and Jean-Claude Passeron, *Reproduction in Education, Society, and Culture* (London: Sage, 1977), 9.

14. Raymond Williams, quoted in Michael W. Apple, *Ideology and Curriculum* (London: Routledge & Kegan Paul, 1979), 6; and Chandra Mukerji and Michael Schudson, eds., "Base and Superstructure in Marxist Cultural Theory," in *Rethinking Popular Culture* (Berkeley: University of California Press, 1991), 414. Williams's

concept of "selective tradition" refers to "that which, within the terms of an effective dominant culture, is always passed off as '*the* tradition,' '*the* significant past.' But always the selectivity is the point; the way in which from a whole possible area of past and present, certain meanings and practices are chosen for emphasis, certain other meanings and practices are neglected and excluded. Even more crucially, some of these meanings and practices are reinterpreted, diluted, or even put into forms which support or at least do not contradict other elements within the effective dominant culture."

15. Steven Seidman, *Contested Knowledge* (Cambridge, Mass.: Blackwell, 1994), 235.

16. See David John Frank, Evan Schofer, and John Charles Torres, "Rethinking History: Change in the University Curriculum: 1910–90," *Sociology of Education* 67 (October 1994): 231–42, on institutionalized redefinitions and alternative curricular constructions.

17. Frances FitzGerald, *America Revised* (Boston: Little, Brown, 1997), 97. Also see James W. Loewen, *Lies My Teacher Told Me* (New York: New Press, 1995); Robert Lerner, Althea K. Nagai, and Stanley Rothman, *Molding the Good Citizen* (Westport, Conn: Praeger, 1995); Philip G. Altbach, Gail P. Kelly, Hugh G. Petrie, and Lois Weis, eds., *Textbooks in American Society* (Albany, N.Y.: SUNY Press, 1991); and Theresa Perry and James W. Fraser, eds., *Freedom's Plow* (New York: Routledge, 1993).

18. See Daniel Liston, "Have We Explained the Relationship between Curriculum and Capitalism? An Analysis of the Selective Tradition," *Educational Theory* 34, no. 2 (Summer 1984): 249; Michael W. Apple, *Official Knowledge* (New York: Routledge, 1993), 67. Apple writes: "The State, like civil society, is a site of *interclass* struggle and negotiation, 'a sphere of political action where the interests of dominant classes [and gendered and racial groups] can be partially institutionalized and realized' as well."

See also Martin Carnoy and Henry M. Levin, *Schooling and Work in the Democratic State* (Stanford, Calif.: Stanford University Press, 1985), 5. The authors argue: "Even as schools attempt to satisfy their mandate within a capitalist economy, the public as a whole and social movements such as the civil rights and women's movements have made them more democratic and equal than other social institutions."

19. Apple, *Official Knowledge*, 68.

20. Apple, *Official Knowledge*, 68.

21. Nathan Glazer, *We Are All Multiculturalists Now* (Cambridge, Mass.: Harvard University Press, 1997), 4. Although Glazer makes this point with a strong sense of resignation, he nonetheless asserts that multiculturalism has triumphed.

# Cultural Politics and Institutional Practice in Texas

## TEXTBOOK BATTLES

I'm here today because I'm concerned about women being maligned for wanting to be homemakers, wives, and mothers. I'm not against career women or women who want careers, but I feel like the other side should be presented. I'm not sure what the definition of a fundamentalist is; but if it's someone who believes in the traditional values that have made America the greatest nation in the history of the world, then I must be a fundamentalist.[1]

In 1985, Carolyn Galloway, mother of two children in Texas public schools, appeared in Austin to testify before the state's textbook selection committee that adopts schoolbooks used in classrooms across the state. Standing at a podium in a large fluorescent-lit board room, Galloway spoke passionately about how her children's textbooks contradicted traditional American values. The selection committee listened patiently to Galloway and many others, asking questions very infrequently and seldom taking notes. I later asked a former committee member what he thought about the testimony he heard at these proceedings. His response typified the feelings of most committee members with whom I spoke.

The bottom line is that there is too much controversy over the textbooks, as if the information in them is going to be indelibly imprinted on the minds of the students forever. The textbook is a tool in the hand of the teacher. The teacher can reinforce or make light of the material as to undermine what is written.[2]

School textbooks are a principal source of knowledge in public schools and they have long been a focus of educational reform and contestation. In the 1930s, Columbia University professor Harold Rugg's progressive social studies textbooks drew active opposition from the National Association of Manufacturers for "supposedly promoting 'Marxist teachings.' "[3] Decades later, in the 1960s and 1970s, minority groups identified cultural and gender biases in textbooks and sought to increase coverage of minority experiences and contributions. In the 1980s, textbooks became a vehicle for New Right agendas.[4] And by the 1990s, schoolbooks were being criticized from both the Right and the Left. James Loewen's book, *Lies My Teacher Told Me,* and Robert Lerner, Althea Nagai, and Stanley Rothman's, *Molding the Good Citizen*, offered conflicting perspectives on persistent myths and misrepresentations in American history textbooks while parents and critics in Oakland, California, rejected a state-adopted social studies book because it was "not multicultural enough."[5]

When groups mobilize to shape textbook knowledge, they do so because they expect this knowledge to validate and legitimate their worldviews. These worldviews reflect fundamentally different ideas about the purpose of school knowledge, its effects on young people, and its role in supporting or transforming the cultural values, norms, and institutions of society. The very nature of textbook protests, their focus on omissions, biases, and perspectives, stems from activists' basic sense that school knowledge is not neutral.

Observers of symbolic crusades use the concept of "status politics" to explain why social groups engage in various forms of cultural struggle. Analyses of temperance crusades and antipornography campaigns, for example, have attributed these movements to repressed status anxieties over lost prestige and the declining legitimacy of traditional values.[6] Ann Page and Donald Clelland interpreted textbook disputes in Kanawha County, West Virginia, during the 1970s, as battles between cultural fundamentalists and cosmopolitans over lifestyle preferences.[7] But while curricular struggles also reflect symbolic meanings, it is important to recognize what else is at stake. These debates are not just about values nor are they just about social status. Rather, they represent conflicts between particular systems of classification and fundamental ways of categorizing reality and the individual.

While my purpose in this chapter is to describe how combatants in textbook battles view the functions of school knowledge as well as the contexts in which they make their views known, I will emphasize that, regardless of their competing perspectives, they treat knowledge as a repository of meanings and ideas and a source of cultural and social stability or change. Although this point will seem self-evident, its significance lies in the fact that those who actually make decisions about knowledge operate according to a very different set of assumptions. The comments of activists reveal what they think, but they also set the stage for contrasting the politics of knowledge with a process of decision making that diffuses conflicts over ideology and contains the impact of public activism.

## TEXTBOOK ADOPTION IN TEXAS

More than 130 years ago, Texas established a centralized process of textbook evaluation and distribution. Its primary purpose was to make instructional materials uniformly accessible to all local school districts in the state.[8] Little did state planners know, however, that by the 1960s the state's textbook adoption system would gain a reputation as one of the most influential sites of educational conflict in the country.

While state textbook adoption is an annual process, books for specific subject areas are adopted in six-year cycles. The following description of the main activities of the adoption process, its key actors, and decision-making points pertain to the system in place from the early 1960s through the mid-1980s when struggles over diversity were prominent. Since the mid-1980s, when I attended hearings and interviewed participants in the process, several components of the adoption system have changed, and these changes are listed in the endnotes of this chapter.[9]

In January of the year preceding the actual selection of books, the Texas State Board of Education would meet to approve textbook content requirements called proclamations. Formulated by the curricular division of the Texas Education Agency (TEA), the proclamations prescribed the knowledge and skills books must include.[10] So, for example, when the state planned to adopt U.S. history textbooks in 1985, the state board of education had already begun reviewing content requirements for history texts in January of 1984. After hearing public comments on the proclamation in February, the board approved a final version in March that was then made available to publishers who planned to offer their books for sale the following year. Typically eight to ten publishers would submit books for a subject area though the exact number of submissions varied by subject matter and size of student enrollment.

In January of the following year (1985 in this example), the adoption cycle resumed and the commissioner of education solicited nominations for candidates to serve on the State Textbook Selection Committee, a fifteen-member group of teachers, superintendents, curriculum specialists, and other professional educators whose primary responsibility was to recommend a list of texts for state approval.[11] In April, those selected to serve would select groups of local advisors, usually other educators but occasionally laypersons, who would assist with the evaluation process. From May through June, committee members and their advisors would meet with sales representatives from publishing companies. Meanwhile, publishers were required to provide copies of their books to the education agency and to regional service centers throughout the state for public review. Interested parties, called "petitioners," would submit their textbook evaluations as "bills of particulars." The Texas Education Agency would then distribute the bills of particulars to textbook committees and publishers.

In July, petitioners testified at public hearings before the state textbook committee, and publishers responded to petitioners' testimony and bills of particulars at the hearings and/or in writing within twenty-one days after the close of the hearings. The state textbook committee reconvened in late August to recommend its list of books for each subject area.

In November, the Texas State Board of Education would hear testimony from petitioners before approving a final list of adopted books. The board could remove books from the textbook committee's recommended list as long as two choices remained available to local school districts. Although the board could not add books to the list, it could replace a text with one the committee had approved as an alternate. In December, the state informed local school districts which textbooks they could purchase with state funds.

In the next section, I focus on the participation of petitioners in the adoption process in order to present their competing claims and conceptions of school knowledge. I then analyze the ways in which the state managed ideological struggle.

## BATTLES OVER SCHOOLBOOK KNOWLEDGE

I feel that some of the history books up for adoption threaten the traditional family values that I hold dear. I realize that our country has gone through some revolutionary changes in views of women, but these books do not represent the other side of the coin when it comes to a woman's role in our society.

You may agree or disagree, but our children should have the other side presented to them as an option so that young girls don't feel put down, unenlightened or unfulfilled if they choose to stay home with their children. They need to see that equality does not depend upon economic equality, a high-paying position or a prestigious job.[12]

Like Carolyn Galloway, Ada Ferguson appeared at the 1985 state hearings to protest textbook depictions of homemakers. Textbooks, she argued, portrayed women who chose to stay at home as less accomplished than their employed peers and implied that homemaking was no longer a legitimate and worthwhile choice. Ferguson's testimony sustained a debate that had been taking place since the early 1970s when publishers began to include more girls in elementary school readers and more female celebrities in history and social studies texts. Responding to social changes initiated by the women's movement, publishers directed their editors and authors to "break job stereotypes," to show "married women who work outside the home," and to portray women and girls as "independent, active, strong, courageous, competent, decisive, persistent, serious-minded, and successful."[13] Textbook authors, they advised, should show heightened sensitivity to language and biases and avoid stereotypes such as "scatterbrained female, fragile flower, goddess on a pedestal, catty gossip, henpecking shrew, apron-wearing mother, frustrated spinster, ladylike little girl."[14]

These efforts to diversify images of women prompted a backlash from groups whose perspective exemplifies what I call a "traditionalist" response to textbook changes. Though traditionalists are often associated with dominant norms and values, by the early 1970s, they saw themselves as challenging the hegemony of a liberal, progressive establishment and claimed to be seeking equal time for their beliefs. In Texas, the Daughters of the American Revolution, the United Daughters of the Confederacy, the Eagle Forum, and Mel and Norma Gabler, a couple from Longview who nearly made a career of reviewing textbooks over the course of twenty-five years, challenged the treatment of women's experiences from a strictly feminist point of view. Textbooks, they suggested were emphasizing Gloria Steinem and the Equal Rights Amendment while censoring Phyllis Schlafly.[15]

Traditionalist groups were equally resistant to the inclusion of racial minorities.[16] Textbook attention to these groups, the Gablers argued, exceeded their historical importance so much so that publishers were presenting new knowledges at the expense of white Americans.[17] The Gablers wrote:

> To sensationalize and overemphasize slavery and racial conflict as portrayed in these texts only reinforces the old stereotyped historical image of the Negro

that is degrading and which makes him ashamed of being black. We question the benefit gained by the kind of lip service to black history that included minor or relatively unimportant episodes and black Americans who made only insignificant contributions to American progress while censoring the names of greater men.[18]

Contesting one textbook description of W. E. B. DuBois as "a brilliant, dignified and angry scholar," another 1972 petitioner attempted to discredit DuBois by claiming that the book failed "to mention the undenied fact that he was also a Communist, who joined the Party quite openly in 1961. . . . So much did DuBois do for Communist causes that they named their youth movement after him—the W. E. B. DuBois Clubs."[19] For traditionalists, previously excluded groups and behaviors might be included but only if textbooks presented them as less legitimate quantitatively and qualitatively. Union activities could be discussed, but only if they were portrayed as a source of civil disorder. Other societies might be described, but only if textbooks highlighted their social and economic problems. Drug use and homosexuality could be addressed, as long as students were told they were wrong.

Seeking a positive and optimistic portrait of American history and identity, traditionalists opposed publishers' efforts not only to expand their treatment of racial minorities, but also to present narratives about social injustice, inequality, and discrimination. As these issues became more prominent in texts by the late 1970s, traditionalists bemoaned the shift from patriotic stories to social problems. One petitioner wrote, "The words 'anti-foreign, anti-Catholic, and anti-black . . . long casting a shadow on American democracy' are 'dismal.' "[20] By emphasizing poverty and urban decline, the Gablers hypothesized, textbooks would incite young students to rebellion.

> Psychologists tell us that a child continually told about his problems, faults, and shortcomings will tend to conform and become this type of person. . . . Yet this text, offered for Texas schools, overwhelmingly emphasizes problems, faults and shortcomings of the United States of America. This is a form of behavioral conditioning that CANNOT FAIL to destroy patriotism in violation of Policy 3331.3(3)b and will condition children to ACCEPT social strife, to disregard the law, and to contribute disorder in violation of Policy 3331.3(3).[21]

As suggested in the reference to "behavioral conditioning," pedagogical innovations that had gained popularity in the classroom climate of the 1960s became a primary target of traditionalist protests. Described by some as "a microcosm of democracy-in-action," social studies classrooms were increasingly influenced by inquiry methods.[22] In some states, the teaching of history "focused on problem solving, decision making, and social action" or was replaced with "multicultural studies, ethnic studies, consumer affairs, and ecology."[23] As classroom activities such as role playing and hypothetical situations became increasingly influential, traditionalists declared that "a student cannot help becoming frustrated with a continuing emphasis on problems and on questions, especially open-ended questions."[24] By shifting educational objectives from the mastery of facts to the free exploration of values, schools, traditionalists felt, were not only neglecting their role as disseminators of "official" knowledge, they were also teaching a hidden curriculum, one that presented school knowledge as neutral while supporting, or at least failing to question, ideas that contradicted Christian beliefs. The Gablers made the following claim:

> At one time American textbooks were almost completely Christian and/or moral, but it is well known that Christianity was removed from textbooks on the pretext that the State has no right or authority to teach religion. Since morality is basically a religious matter, the removal of morality followed on the premise that texts should be "neutral." But note that the vacuum of morality in the texts has been and is being filled with content that reeks of sex, crime, drugs, civil disobedience, lawbreaking, violence, rebellion. Failure to teach moral implication in human action and relationships is to convey an acceptance of these other things as being the "norms," rather than problems to be corrected.[25]

To traditionalists, inquiry approaches and other new instructional models promoted cultural and moral relativism. These petitioners found support for their beliefs in works such as Schlafly's *Child Abuse in the Classroom*. By asking students to reveal personal feelings and to question their parents' values, schools, Schlafly argued, we are violating individual rights to privacy and threatening the authority of the family and community.

## PROGRESSIVE KNOWLEDGE
## AND PEDAGOGY

Though equally concerned about textbook messages and misrepresentations, proponents of a "progressive" view of school knowledge advocated a fundamentally different perspective. They, too, focused on the quantitative and qualitative representation of topics in history. But in contrast to traditionalists' claims that publishers were paying too much

attention to the women's movement, progressive groups such as Texas
NOW (National Organization for Women) and the Texas Women's
Political Caucus[26] argued that history textbooks devoted only a small
proportion of text to women, ignored "noble and famous women," and
mentioned women "only in relation to the men around them, rather
than with reference to their own capabilities."[27] Dismayed that books
were portraying women in a very limited number of occupations, one
representative asserted that publishers were reinforcing stereotypes.

> A young female student in high school would be hard-pressed to find a female
> model to identify with or look up to as reported here unless she was aspiring to
> be a queen, an entertainer, or a Social Worker. There are no women lawyers,
> professionals, educators, athletes, doctors, politicians or historians reported.
> We demand that more affirmative action be taken and until that affirmative
> action is done, we recommend the rejection of this book as it is.[28]

While most textbooks had begun to include the achievements of
individual women, feminist groups found that the books tended to
decontextualize women's issues, exaggerate the extent to which gender
equality had been achieved, and neglect the broader group struggles of
which individual accomplishments were a part. Describing the content
of *Perspectives in U.S. History*, one reviewer wrote:

> Women are given, both as individuals and as a cultural group, cursory and
> token treatment. Of the entire book, women are mentioned on eighteen
> pages. Ms. Mott receives one reference, and Ms. Steinem one line under a
> picture. Those few paragraphs that attempt to discuss the women's movement
> treat it as a social phenomenon, not a movement rooted in economic, legal,
> social, and political discrimination.[29]

Textbook critiques from progressive women's groups clearly offered
a counterpoint to traditionalist claims; however, the aims of these
groups were rather modest. When textbooks began to depict women in
a greater variety of activities by the late 1970s, NOW representatives
halted their participation in the textbook hearings. According to NOW
representative Marjorie Randal, publishers were finally addressing the
kinds of changes her group had been looking for. "By that time [1979],
there was almost nothing to complain about," she said. "If we wanted
to complain, we would've had to move to a far more sophisticated
level. There was still plenty to say about what was wrong with the
books from a sexist point of view. But they had at least caught up with
the ideas that we had started out with."[30]

It was not until the mid-1980s that other progressive groups revived the focus on women's issues and pressed for further change. In 1985, Broader Perspectives, a progressive organization in Houston, praised textbook images[31] of women branding cattle and working in factories as well as a special feature on photographer Frances Johnston, and "a wonderful explanation of how sex discrimination came to be part of the Civil Rights Act of 1964."[32] Nonetheless, Elizabeth Judge, the group's director, found persistent weaknesses as well. Among other shortcomings, textbooks still gave too little attention to women's suffrage[33] and to women's participation in the First and Second World Wars.[34] By identifying more subtle biases in the treatment of women and men, and by expanding its review process to include racial minorities, Broader Perspectives sought to move beyond the agendas of NOW.

## AFFIRMING RACIAL AND ETHNIC DIVERSITY

While traditionalists argued that textbooks exaggerated the significance of minority group struggles, progressive groups countered that textbooks were not doing enough to challenge ignorance, racism, and discrimination. In contrast to the traditionalist claim that textbooks gave too much attention to blacks in the military, Broader Perspectives noted "no mention of the racial conflict that Black troops faced in the U.S."[35] Several books, the group discovered, did not use the term Holocaust, "or mention that there were 12 million victims, 6 million of which were Jewish."[36]

The organization also identified numerous ways in which textbooks perpetuated stereotypes and blamed the victim.[37]

Cite [from textbook]: "Black contributions." . . . Like Indians, black Americans by their very presence in the colonies forced the settlers to develop new social arrangements. Slavery compelled the colonists to create methods of controlling the labor and the lives of other human beings. It confronted all the colonists, particularly the slave owners, with a moral problem that they were unable to solve except by the irrational declaration that Africans were inferior people.
Comment [from petitioner]: These statements are factually true. (One could say that the presence of Jews forced Hitler to develop new social arrangements and so forth.) This is a clear case of 'blame the victim' for the situation. It gives no one but the victim the responsibility for slavery as though slavery just happened because the Africans were there. To add insult to injury, these statements are placed under the heading of 'Black contributions' which, like

'Indian contributions' acknowledges people only insofar as they contributed to the colonies.[38]

One book portrayed Chinese immigrants as "our most orderly and industrious citizens." Contesting the stereotypical account, Broader Perspectives noted, "When the Chinese organized a strike on the railroad for higher wages and an end to whipping, they were starved out by the railroad company. The extreme of 'orderly and industrious' was something forced upon them."[39]

In contrast to the Texas Daughters of the American Revolution whose representative objected to photos of Langston Hughes and Malcolm X because they "were each 16 times larger than any photograph of George Washington,"[40] People for the American Way (PFAW), a civil liberties group founded by television producer Norman Lear,[41] appeared at textbook hearings in the mid-1980s to highlight tokenistic representations of minorities. One reviewer for the group wrote:

> This textbook contains 528 pages. Only four paragraphs are devoted to Hispanic Americans, a group whose population now exceeds 14 million. The valuable contributions and the role that Hispanics have played in shaping American history merit more attention. To feature a picture of golfer Nancy Lopez (p. 482), while it pays homage to her accomplishments, does little to redress the wrong. American Indians, Blacks, and women are allotted similar minimum coverage.[42]

In addition, PFAW argued that textbooks continued to present a sterilized view of race relations. By making this claim, the organization attempted to shift its focus from ethnic group representation to a more critical analysis of intergroup conflict. Reviewers wrote:

> There is a pervasive indication that although some misguided Americans may have directed hostilities at certain minorities, the dominant groups in the United States have learned their lesson and led the way in shaping a truly democratic and egalitarian society.[43]

In sum, according to two progressive groups most active in state hearings during the 1980s, textbook presentations of women and minority groups had expanded but remained seriously flawed. Not only did textbooks fail to portray America as a culturally pluralistic society, they also neglected to equip students with the knowledge that would move them toward active participation in social critique and social change.

## MAKING CRITICAL CITIZENS

The views of traditionalist and progressive groups differed with respect to the purpose of school knowledge as well as to issues of representation and inclusion. While traditionalists proclaimed that schools must teach absolute values, present knowledge as facts, and promote patriotism, progressives viewed school knowledge as a source of liberation and young people as future citizens who must learn to be independent, tolerant, critical thinkers. Traditionalists argued that students are children in need of rules and instruction; by contrast, progressives advanced an equally sacred view of the individual as an active, contesting person. One representative of NOW explained the value of role-playing activities this way:

> If you're doing role playing and you're asking people to make choices about which is right or which is wrong, that is certainly the purpose of education. I can't imagine that that would be an infringement on the privacy of the student or on the parents' role because it seems to me that parenting does involve presenting, certainly my model of the parent and perhaps one that's shared by many people, or hopefully is, is to encourage the child to develop values through the discussion and presentation of alternative perspectives.
>
> And so I don't see that as infringing on the right to privacy. It does seem to me that the most important thing a teacher can do in this situation is to not allow the social pressures in the classroom to impinge upon a student who takes a position that may be considered unconventional.[44]

Rema Lou Brown, also a representative of NOW and a former schoolteacher, described how she taught her students to question the material presented in their textbooks.

> So one day, the kids had to bring their textbook, and an indelible pencil with permanent ink. No ballpoints. And we went through a chapter that I just chose at random, and said "all right, we're going to underline editorial opinion, and there's nothing wrong with editorial opinion but you've got a right to know it's there and recognize and quarrel with it." . . . And my first test to those kids was a paragraph in which they were to draw out the facts, draw out the interpretations, and draw out any misrepresentation of the facts that could be biased. I wanted to teach them how to think, not what to think, and to teach them they could quarrel with anyone. There is nothing wrong with arguing, if you have information that is in conflict with the information you're being given. I don't care if it's me, stand up and say, "Ms. Brown, now I have read . . ." and cite your source, and "I'd like to know how . . ." and finish your sentence.[45]

While traditionalists opposed textbook references to social conflict, progressive groups criticized publishers for avoiding controversial issues such as affirmative action and busing.[46] Civics education, the latter maintained, must foster critical and analytical skills. PFAW, for example, denounced watered-down textbook knowledge because the material provided little means of understanding distinct points of view.

> For the most part, our reviewers found that these books are solid works of scholarship—thorough, current, informed. . . . But our reviewers agree that many of the books have a common, major deficiency. While they are impressive collections of facts, they are intellectually and pedagogically dull tools for inspiring effective participation in the democratic political process. Many of the books are largely disembodied expositions of principles and facts, lacking the passion of the conflicts that infuse politics and government with meaning and significance.
>
> The problem is less with the individual books than in their general didactic approach. The student is asked only to master knowledge of the subject rather than to put this knowledge to use. Thus, the participatory side, the side that requires the individual to analyze democratic values, processes, and choices, is largely ignored.[47]

The group encouraged textbooks that challenged students to use "imaginative thinking, both in formulating questions and discovering creative solutions."[48] Consistent with the ideals of radical progressive theorists, they treated school knowledge in general, and social studies in particular, as potential sources of critical literacy. Hence, they defined civic education not as lessons about loyalty, patriotism, and morality, as traditionalists suggested, but rather, as a basis of individual and group empowerment.

Together, traditionalist and progressive views captured both the enthusiasm for and the backlash against multiple perspectives and a more inclusive model of American identity. From the 1960s to the mid-1980s, efforts to move textbook knowledge in a progressive direction were clearly resisted by those seeking to maintain a single version of history and society. However, despite the disagreements between these competing groups, the interests of petitioners as a whole also indicate a common approach to evaluating textbook knowledge, one that paid attention specifically to its meanings, its messages, and its potential impact on young people. To contrast this approach with what was most valued in the process of choosing textbooks, I now examine the significance of public mobilizations within the institutional context of textbook adoption.

## THE INSTITUTIONALIZATION OF
## PUBLIC PARTICIPATION

Reporters from local news agencies regularly attended the textbook hearings; they cited petitioners' testimonies in their coverage of proceedings especially when controversial views were aired. Yet, despite the passion with which petitioners presented their claims and the media attention they received, the intensity and substance of their battles over official knowledge were moderated through the institutional practices of bureaucratic democracy.[49] The organization of the adoption process, the allocation of authority, the bases of decision making largely restricted the impact of cultural politics on decisions about official knowledge. Contrary to models of elite control, the public had a right to articulate its claims; however, contrary to models of contestation and counterhegemony, there was no guarantee that its requests or ideas would be part of the decision-making process.[50] The inclusion of citizens' input legitimized the state's position as a site of democratic pluralism while simultaneously ensuring that cultural politics were contained.

Textbook adoption in Texas is a highly structured and routinized process. While petitioners could and did offer volumes of textbook reviews and testimony at state proceedings, they had no formal authority to decide which textbooks were chosen or if and how the content of selected books would be revised. Indeed, their claims could make an impact only if publishers, textbook committee members, and state board officials believed their comments were important and used them in their decision-making processes.[51]

Several features of the process lessened the effects of petitioners' testimony on these decision makers' actions. Generally, textbook adoption practices are classified according to two types of political processes, a form of "institutionalized politics" through which educators, publishers, and administrators carry out tasks designated by the state, and "deinstitutionalized politics" by which pressure groups exercise influence outside the formal evaluation and selection of textbooks.[52] In the latter case, interest groups presumably have an impact insofar as they make ideological conflicts public, gain the attention of the news media, and protest in ways that require arbitration by higher authorities.[53]

However, the Texas process has always been something of a hybrid; it institutionalizes public mobilizations by combining features of both models, yet subordinating the second model to the first. In other words, it invites public input, but through its structure of authority and the logistics by which petitioners present their views, it regulates how, when, and the terms under which input is received. Time allotted for testimony, for instance, decreased from unlimited time in the 1960s to two hours in the early seventies. By 1978, the state allowed each petitioner twelve minutes per textbook. In 1986, it reduced testimony to ten minutes per subject area, which amounts to a very brief opportunity to speak given that a petitioner could conceivably review ten or more books per subject.

The organization of the process weakened petitioners' potential influence as well. State textbook committees heard petitioners' testimony after they and their advisors had already formed opinions about which books to select. Similarly, publishers listened to testimony after they had produced their books, and the state board of education heard testimony about textbook content at the end of the adoption process. In theory, Texas citizens might successfully pressure state board members who have been elected to represent their congressional districts.[54] In practice, the channel of influence is far from direct. State board elections attract relatively few voters, and there is little evidence that candidates are asked how they might vote on decisions pertaining to textbook adoptions. Campaigns for election most commonly address issues of school finance, extracurricular activities, and broad curricular reforms. For example, the state's no-pass, no-play rule for student athletes garnered much more attention in the mid-1980s than did controversies over textbooks.

While board members sometimes deliberated over issues of content, these discussions related only occasionally to the types of arguments petitioners made. Rejecting a book that the textbook committee recommended was an exception, not a rule. Generally the Texas state boards I observed rubber stamped the committee's recommendations, a pattern attributable to the board's lack of expertise in the field of education. State boards have included former senators, lawyers, physicians, and corporate executives, few of whom have had the capacity or incentive to systematically review the books themselves.

## THE POWER OF PROFESSIONAL AUTHORITY

A second mitigating factor is the dual logic with which petitioners and decision makers approached the meaning of textbook knowledge. As noted previously, when parents and interest groups have mobilized to contest what schools teach, they have treated textbook knowledge as a source of worldviews, values, and morals. Parents see themselves as guardians of truth; they are concerned about what messages their children are receiving, what values are being legitimated, and whether these are consistent with their own versions of reality. Despite the fact that interest groups articulate contradictory perspectives, they view school knowledge in terms of its cultural and social implications.

In contrast, decision makers approach school knowledge quite differently. Texas textbook committees composed primarily of teachers, curriculum experts, and administrators recommend the books that will be offered to local districts for adoption.[55] Typically the committees I observed selected five books from ten to fifteen choices in each subject area for which the state was adopting books. Even though the state board of education had the authority to reject some of the committee's choices, the latter's responsibility of narrowing the list was very important.

I interviewed twenty-nine educators who served on state textbook committees between 1966 and 1986,[56] and observed interactions among committees and between committee members and petitioners at public hearings in 1985 and 1986. I found that in addition to the institutional mechanisms that regulated public mobilizations, both textbook selection committees and schoolbook publishers largely dismissed what parents and interest groups had to say.

## TEXAS STATE TEXTBOOK COMMITTEE HEARINGS

At the textbook hearings held in July of each year, members of the textbook selection committee sat at individual desks, facing one another in a circle. In front of the circle, as one entered the room, was a podium from which petitioners testified, and behind the podium was a section of chairs where petitioners waited until they were called to speak. To the right of the circle and along the right wall of the room, representatives of publishing companies, the media, and other observers occupied several rows of chairs.

In theory, the hearings offered an opportunity for the textbook committee to engage in dialogue with petitioners and among themselves about specific matters of textbook content. Following each petitioner's testimony, committee members were invited to ask questions pertaining to the testimony or to bills of particulars submitted earlier in the spring. Before the hearings in July 1985, I had examined most of the bills of particulars offered, some of which were voluminous. Thus, what struck me most about the hearings was the lack of reaction to petitioners' testimony. Despite the earnestness with which they spoke, their views and opinions generated little interest or discussion among the textbook committee members. The latter certainly appeared to listen; however, rarely did they comment on petitioners' points of view or ask them to elaborate on their positions and provide further information or clarification.

Interviews with committee members illuminated several reasons for their seeming disinterest in the kinds of concerns petitioners raised—are textbook materials biased, what impressions do they create, what information do they leave out? On the one hand, committee members acknowledged the public's right to make their views known; some even felt appreciative of occasions when citizens or groups identified errors and problems they and their advisors had overlooked. For example, Pamela Neely, who served in 1972, described the favorable impact of feminist groups as follows:

> Of course some of that is needed to be, and has brought change, and has awakened people. . . . I don't know that I had thought about it beforehand, really, that every time they had a kid playin' ball [in a textbook] or playin' something (and here I am in physical education), it was always a little boy. I guess that never, that was never a big thing to me, until they [feminist groups] pointed that out.

On the other hand, most members rejected laypersons' views because they believed petitioners took material out of context and made claims that were fanatic or "way out in left field." Some committee members had difficulty taking petitioners' claims seriously, such as Phyllis Lee who recalled:

> I thought some of the people were utterly ridiculous. Now, some had good points. And it's nice that they all got to have their say. But they didn't have any influence whatsoever on my voting.

Reflecting on their interpretations of petitioners' input, several members remembered feeling that parents, interest groups, and critical theorists exaggerated the significance of textbook material in the learning process. Dale Clyde, a high school principal, explained:

> In '78, there was so much, nineteen or twenty volumes of protests, and you and I both know that you're not going to read all that. To be honest, I didn't read but about three pages of that junk. It was like a rite of passage [for peti-

tioners]. They knew that they had to write something in order to speak. Most of the fanatics spoke. . . . They were regarded almost unanimously by the professionals as a bunch of jokers.

Committee members expressed a common impression that petitioners mistakenly viewed the textbook as the sole source of classroom information. Petitioners, they felt, tended to overestimate the textbook's impact on the learning process and to ignore the role of individual teachers in transmitting material. Clyde further explained:

> We were looking at something closer to what the state wanted. The protestors were looking at different things. When we left the hearings, we would say, "these people must think there's no teacher in the classroom," that the teachers say, "here's the book, read it, and never forget it for the rest of your life." We never took that stock in the textbook itself like those protestors did. They acted as if one bad sentence corrupts a whole generation.

Textbook selection committees did not expect to find a perfect textbook and assumed that teachers will elaborate upon sections of books that are underdeveloped or one-sided. Social studies teachers, several members noted, also rely on more than textbooks; they use a variety of supplementary resources including newspapers and periodicals in their classrooms. The extent to which most classroom teachers do fulfill these expectations is, of course, questionable. Teachers selected to serve on textbook committees are among the most talented and energetic of their profession; their behaviors are probably atypical. Nonetheless, despite acknowledging that teachers with less experience might depend more heavily on textbooks, these educators felt that most teachers exercised a great deal of independence and used materials selectively as part of a broader, individualized plan of instruction.

## OBJECTIVITY AND PEDAGOGY

How committee members characterized petitioners' claims reveals much about the distinction they made between the concerns of experts and the claims of activists. While petitioners politicized educational content, committee members saw textbook knowledge as having no implicit or explicit political messages. From their perspective, it was only when activists, from the Left or the Right, read too much into the material that knowledge *became* a subject of controversy and cultural struggle.

While petitioners came to the textbook hearings to engage in debates about ideas and perspectives, these matters were not only beyond the scope of, but also inconsistent with, the committee's responsibility to focus on educational criteria, which, according to those committee members interviewed, were clearly distinguishable from "philosophical concerns." The latter viewed themselves as professional experts who must not be swayed by public passions and political interests. Instead of settling debates over conflicting ideas and beliefs, they intended to separate pedagogical issues from values, politics, and social interests, and thought they could do so even though the ideology of professional expertise is itself political.

This assumption is reflected in the comments of Ann Simmons, a high school English teacher.

> Most of the testimony I remember fell into two big groups. But quite a bit of the testimony had nothing to do with *what we were supposed to judge the books on* [author's emphasis]. To me they were mostly personal prejudices. But there was nothing in their comments. . . . they didn't affect me at all.
>
> It is a good idea to have them. You never know, somebody could bring up something really worthwhile. People should have a chance to voice their opinions. Of course, when the public starts talking about George Washington's picture [being too small], I can't see that that has any bearing on anything. And that was the caliber of most of the comments. Very few of those people addressed the types of things on our lists.

Hence, while the relative size of Malcolm X's and George Washington's pictures was a bone of contention for textbook protestors, these issues and their political implications were of low caliber to textbook committees who treated them as being outside the realm of bureaucratic, professional decision making.

On the one hand, we may rest assured that educators were not easily swayed by extreme pressures to reject textbooks on the basis of one picture. On the other hand, we might be legitimately concerned that evaluators regarded specific content matters as "small things." For while the attempt to separate ideological issues from the performance of professional and bureaucratic tasks creates an appearance of neutrality, avoiding issues of substance is not the same as being objective about them. Rather, technical concerns mask social and political interests. As theorist Alvin Gouldner once wrote:

> It is not correct to say that technology *becomes* the new ideology and replaces ideology; rather it *represses* the ideological problem and inhibits ideological creativity and adaptation.[57]

Summarizing the consequences for decision making, he concluded:

> The development of a technocracy has not simply crippled the possibilities of *democratic* control. The technocracy has, also, greatly limited the effective exercise of power even by those in *control* of the bureaucratic organization. It is not simply the "man in the street" but the hegemonic classes and elites themselves whose power is now limited, even though it enhances their legitimacy, to the extent that they proclaim their decisions to be governed by scientific considerations.[58]

In chapter 3, I further analyze the implications of technocratic rationality for the selection of knowledge and for professional autonomy. The point here is that neutrality and educational imperatives were the primary rationales textbook committees offered to explain their attitudes toward petitioners. I turn now to publishers' perceptions of public mobilizations to document a similar pattern of response.

## "THAT'S MY STORY AND I'M STICKIN' TO IT"

If public mobilizations functioned to promote or inhibit ideological changes in textbook content, we would expect publishers to feel pressured by interest groups and attempt to accommodate their demands. However, by and large, these mobilizations do not affect the content of school knowledge as dramatically or obviously as is believed.

Several publishing representatives I interviewed acknowledged that in the late 1960s and early 1970s, some petitioners appeared to have some impact.[59] For example, Henry Graham, who was a textbook sales representative during this period, said that his company catered to the Gablers' interests because it feared their protests might sway the decisions of the Texas State Board of Education.

> We were submitting a psychology text in Texas, and I had to make the presentation during the protests, and Mrs. Gabler sat right across the table from me . . . and questioned me about the author's reference to the, he called it the myth of Jonah and the whale. . . . Well, she disliked the word "myth" because she was defending the scriptures fundamentally, and I had to try to disabuse her of that. And she objected to this in the textbook, which was ultimately adopted. But it cost us money. In other words, we had to tailor our textbooks to Texas, and take a big chance that we were going to sell enough of them down there to justify that. We had a warehouse full of books.

In contrast, by the mid-1980s, publishing representatives seemed much less concerned about the presence of petitioners in the textbook adoption process. Tim Peterson, an executive director of social studies for a publishing company, said:

> When the economics books were under criticism by Grusendorf [a former petitioner and state board member] we didn't change anything. The book was adopted and we came in number one. You just sort of weather the storm because the next time around things may have changed. I don't think we sat down and said, "We were attacked on this point, should we consider changing it or doing it differently?" Now if there's a problem of interpretation, we might change a term; it depends on the integrity of the content. If a critic has a legitimate point, yeah, we'll look at it, but only if it is reasonable.

Others argued that although petitioners should be allowed to voice their views, they had very little clout. Shirley Flint, director of her company's social studies department, put it this way:

> So there's nothing about this process that makes us have to tell our authors what to say or what not to say. And I think our authors would all say that's true, that they're not told by editors that they can't say something that they believe is important because it won't fly in Texas.

Indeed, many sales representatives at the state's hearings I attended did not appear worried. Instead, they spent much of their time casually conversing outside the board room with colleagues or former coworkers.[60] When it was their turn to respond to public testimony, most limited their remarks to a standard, near-universal response: "Commissioner . . . members of the textbook committee, we appreciate this opportunity to appear before you. We have responded in writing to the bills of particulars in the 21 day period, and we will stand on those written comments." Their performance seemed ritualistic.

Furthermore, publishers' written responses to the objections of Texas petitioners indicate that they were generally willing to correct dates and typos, but were far less likely to agree with criticisms of substantive content. Like textbook committees, they contended that petitioners misinterpreted seemingly neutral facts or took material out of context. In 1978, publisher Allyn and Bacon provided eighty-seven responses to one Texas petitioner's objections to inquiry approaches to learning. In seventy-five of those responses, the company asserted that her objections were unclear or that she was merely stating her opinion.[61]

When the Gablers argued that Allyn and Bacon's textbook *The People Make a Nation* "overemphasize[d] discrimination, prejudice, and racism to the point where students' own attitudes would become biased," the book's publisher replied,

> It is merely the critics' opinion that our text emphasizes militants, slavery, degradation, hatred, and one minority race. Our text presents a wide cross-section of opinions about slavery and segregation, including the views of slave owners and Southern writers. Unit I of *The People Make A Nation* devotes one or more reading selections to each of the following minority groups other than blacks: Germans, Indians, Scotch-Irish, Scandinavians, Italians, Russians, Poles, Jews, Orientals, and Mexican-Americans. . . . It is our belief that the emphasis of our text on the contributions of all minority groups to the building of America encourages mutual respect and understanding, not hatred.[62]

Publishers typically disagreed with petitioners' interpretations of textbook content or asserted that the book did, in fact, adhere to petitioners' values. However, they rarely defended their material as part of a particular philosophy of education or as a legitimate point of view. For example, Harcourt Brace Jovanovich supported the content of its book *Rise of the American Nation* as follows:

> The work of Langston Hughes is among the most frequently anthologized in all American literature. Hughes was often referred to as "the Poet Laureate of Harlem." He won a Guggenheim Fellowship and a grant from the American Academy of Arts and Letters. The poem quoted on page 180 of the Teacher's Manual is neither pro-Communist nor anti-American. It is critical of discrimination but displays pride and optimism in being black.[63]

When petitioners claimed textbooks were too negative or that they encouraged social strife, publishers simply said their statements were untrue. Again, they were far less likely to assert the importance of learning about social strife. On the contrary, as the following two responses show, representatives of Allyn and Bacon avoided taking a stance on how knowledge should be portrayed.

> Criticism: p. 338, 339 "A Student Manifesto": This article plants the seeds for student unrest and disorder in violation of Policy 3331.3.
> Reply: Part 3 of Unit VIII is about the activities of youth in the 1960s. The fact is that one such activity was student participation in the revision of school codes and curriculum. Students are encouraged to evaluate the example of an actual manifesto on its merits or lack of them. They are never told to accept its proposals.[64]

When the Gablers asserted that the textbook gave too much attention to poverty, Allyn and Bacon replied:

As for poverty, it was a major focus of government attention and popular interest in the 1960s and therefore was given substantial treatment in a unit of the text about this recent decade. The authors have built a constructive and positive unit of materials with examples of poverty, but also with proposed solutions which show hope for the future. The proposed solutions are all based on legal procedures, not on social strife and violation of the law.[65]

To a description of Cesar Chavez as "a power-hungry, unscrupulous man who used threats and violence to control the 'poor farm workers,' " Allyn and Bacon's representative attempted to offer a neutral response:

Reply: The critics have stated their opinion of Cesar Chavez. Our *authors have expressed no opinion of Chavez* [author's emphasis]. The illustration identifies Chavez as a leader of Mexican-American causes, particularly La Huelga. The purpose of this Part 2 of Unit VIII is to illustrate examples of poverty and some of the feelings it arouses, not to condemn or extol leaders of minority groups who seek improved conditions.[66]

Finally, to justify the knowledge they presented, publishers commonly pointed out their adherence to state content requirements. Social studies editor Cheryl Jacobs explained:

Well, you can tell by reading them, I guess, how much they [editors] are willing to bend. If you read through them, you'll see that they'll [petitioners] make one suggestion, and the publisher will perhaps say "we agree with this, and we'll change it," or they might say, "we don't agree with this, and we won't change it." . . . Sometimes people will quote back, they'll use the framework to quote back to them [petitioners], to say that one of the sections that someone objects to is in the framework, and that's why it's in the book. Which is probably not why it's in the book, but it's a very useful way of saying, not "I don't agree with you," but rather, "that's what we're supposed to do."

## IDEOLOGY DENIED AGAIN

Like textbook committee members, publishers ignored the politics of deciding whose knowledge counts. For example, in response to the criticism that textbooks gave insufficient attention to women, Laidlaw Brothers implied that its book *Challenge and Change* simply reflected what had occurred in history:

By the very wealth of history, history texts can recount only a few of the major events in history and whether for the reason Ms. Hickie states or not, women in the past were seldom participants in the historic events that are now selected for inclusion in history texts. In short, it is an author's judgment as to which events will be included in a text. If the events selected did not include women for whatever reason, then there will be fewer women than men in some history books.[67]

"Ms. Hickie's comments are sometimes trite, often not to the point, and illustrate a superficial and not well documented review of the text," Laidlaw concluded.[68] While the publisher acknowledged the importance of an "author's judgment," it proceeded to dismiss the ramifications of this judgment and to minimize the importance of an author's power to choose from a wide range of possible historical figures and events. The response is reminiscent of E. D. Hirsch's argument in his 1988 bestseller *Cultural Literacy.* "By accident of history," he wrote, "American cultural literacy has a bias toward English literate traditions. Short of revolutionary political upheaval, there is absolutely nothing that can be done about this."[69] Likewise, publisher Rand McNally expressed "complete sympathy with the women's rights movement," but offered a similar explanation for the near absence of women in its textbook. According to Rand McNally, *The Adventure of the American People* contained more pictures of men because men had received more public attention and had been sought out by photographers; meanwhile, it included more quotes from men because they had had more opportunities to speak publicly and have their words recorded.[70]

Much like textbook selection committee members, publishers spoke of the knowledge they were transmitting in a very matter-of-fact way, that is, as if controversy were fairly easy to avoid. Janice Gerson, an executive editor of social studies, explained how publishers legitimized their choices.

I can't think of anything really and truly that's ever been left out of a book that I've been involved with or have known about because it bothered a group. You might try and be careful about how you phrase it, and we would be very careful if we knew it was an issue that's going to raise a red flag, to make sure that it was in fact supported, and absolutely accurate, and not allowing any opinions to slip in. But that's more the way it would be handled.

Or if you had a choice you wouldn't talk about . . . but even there, I was going to say a particular person, but social studies were protested for years about including Martin Luther King. And if you did include Martin Luther King, you had to say he was a Communist, you know, those kinds of protests. As far as I know, no one ever left Martin Luther King out, and no one ever said he was a Communist. So the protests were there, and your defense was that this was an accurate statement. Children in Texas are required to learn about the Civil Rights Movement. Martin Luther King was the leader of the Civil Rights Movement, and is an essential part of understanding that history.

Several publishing representatives observed that petitioners' views were sometimes useful. As editor Shirley Flint put it, they "sharpen your wits a bit. . . . I'm the department head," she said. "I read the manuscripts with an eye to whether there are issues of invasion of privacy, and my staff knows that I do that. They're going to be more careful about that. I'm not sure the issue of invasion of privacy would even be there if this [traditionalist protests] hadn't happened." However, despite acknowledging that some progressive teaching methods might be too intrusive, Flint made it clear that her heightened sensitivity did not necessarily mean bowing to traditionalists' claims.

> Well, [there are] always educators who are trying to relate school material to students' own lives. That's just kind of a precept of education. . . . And so you'll often ask students to talk about something in their own lives that's relevant to what you're going to be teaching. . . . But I would agree that there are times when those kinds of suggestions get carried away, and the authors writing them may not really be aware of what it's going to be like for the student in the classroom who is called on by the teacher to make public to the class something that might be private.
>
> And so the fact that those pressure groups were continually criticizing that kind of activity I think has made editors more sensitive. Well, there I think it did have an effect and it was a good one. But it certainly didn't make us as sensitive as some groups would like because they would like that you don't do anything like that [activity] at all. And editors can't . . . not do anything like that at all because it's an important educational method.

Other editors agreed that while they did not begin their staff meetings by asking, "So what was it that petitioners objected to in the last adoption?" they had gained an intuitive feel for what might be objectionable based on their accumulated knowledge of petitions, hearings, and letters protesting their books. Even though they did not cite many instances of direct influence, they did want to avoid risk and they treated interest group claims as one barometer of what is controversial and what the state might reject. Gerson said:

> You'll just be looking at a picture, and if you've done this long enough, you're attuned. . . . You begin to have a sense of what to watch for and what might cause problems. Say you'll be reading something and it just doesn't feel right. You need to tone it down or add a couple more sentences or something because you don't want to get thrown out for something that isn't worth it.

But I really don't think you leave something out that's significant because of interest groups.

In sum, publishers' responses sidestepped the social and political implications of decisions about textbook knowledge. Although they did make efforts to increase the representation of women in history text-books, for example, these changes pertained mainly to issues of writing style (pronouns and adjectives) and illustrations. Publishers did not describe specific ways in which they dealt with matters of interpretation, explored untapped areas of scholarship, or attempted to broaden their discussions of women in history. Their tactics may account for persistent shortcomings identified in more recent texts. In a review of a 1992 world history text, Myra and David Sadker observed:

> In the entire 631 pages of a textbook covering the history of the world, only seven pages related to women, either as famous individuals or as a general group. Two of the seven pages were about Samantha Smith, the fifth-grade Maine student who traveled to the Soviet Union on a piece mission. While we felt that Samantha Smith's story brought an interesting message to other students, we wondered why Susan B. Anthony didn't rate a single line.[71]

## PUBLISHERS' RESISTANCE TO TRANSFORMING KNOWLEDGE

To assess the extent to which publishers responded favorably or unfavorably to petitions from both traditionalist and progressive groups, I examined publishers' responses to petitions in 1972, 1978, 1985, and 1986. I coded responses according to the following categories: defense of substantive material (DS), defense of factual material (DF), agreement with substantive comment (AS), and agreement with factual comment (AF). "Facts" include grammar, spelling, typographical errors, and dates. "Substantive" claims pertained to definitions and meanings, amount of information, and interpretations—all of which involve subjective assessments and not indisputable facts. As indicated in tables 1 and 2 publishers usually defended their textbooks against criticisms from both traditionalist and progressive groups.

However, by the mid-1980s, publishers were almost four times more likely (10.4 percent versus 2.7 percent) to respond positively to all comments than was the case in the 1970s, and they were almost twice as likely (12.6 percent versus 6.9 percent) to agree with the comments of progressive groups. What changed? I attribute their more favorable

**Table 1    Publishers' Responses to Substantive Comments**

| | High School U.S. History Texts (1972 and 1978) | | | | |
| Type of Group | Defend | (%) | Agree | (%) | Total |
|---|---|---|---|---|---|
| Traditionalist | 345 | 97.7 | 8 | 2.3 | 353 |
| Progressive | 160 | 96.4 | 6 | 3.6 | 166 |
| Total | 505 | 97.3 | 14 | 2.7 | 519 |

Source: Texas Education Agency, *Response to Written Comments,* 1972 and 1978 Adoptions.

**Table 2    Publishers' Responses to Substantive Comments**

| | High School U.S. History (1985) and Government Texts (1986) | | | | |
| Type of Group | Defend | (%) | Agree | (%) | Total |
|---|---|---|---|---|---|
| Traditionalist | 487 | 93.1 | 36 | 6.9 | 523 |
| Progressive | 712 | 87.4 | 103 | 12.6 | 815 |
| Total | 1199 | 89.6 | 139 | 10.4 | 1338 |

Source: Texas Education Agency, *Response to Written Comments,* 1985 and 1986 Adoptions.

responses over time not to ideological sympathies, but to the fact that petitioners' comments became somewhat more specific and fact-oriented during the 1980s. Petitioners were requesting more changes in terms and phrases rather than submitting lengthy criticisms about the message of a text. The Gablers' petitions, which constituted a large portion of counterprogressive claims, began to point out specific errors in texts rather than contesting ideological messages. In 1985 and 1986 their petitions accounted for 89.0 percent and 89.9 percent of factual comments agreed with by publishers. Furthermore, in 1985 and 1986, Broader Perspectives accounted for 91.6 percent and 81.5 percent of the substantive claims submitted by all progressive groups. In the adoptions for history and government, the group accounted for 67.3 percent and 78.9 percent of the substantive claims "agreed to" by publishers.

Publishers are more likely to agree to replace or alter brief phrases or specific terms because these do not involve the extensive costs or time commitments that major additions or revisions of material would entail. The following are examples of the types of changes publishers agreed to make:

[Comment]: *History of the American Nation* does not mention . . . the Neutrality Acts of 1935, 1936, and 1937.
[Response]: We will add mention of these acts.[72]

[Comment]:-P.22–23 . . . says that the Chinese immigrants were organized in "highly disciplined" work gangs, but does not mention the discrimination involved, a common omission in texts.
[Reply]: "highly disciplined work gangs"—will be changed to "cruelly disciplined."[73]
[Comment]:-P.198(2) "At the time of his death at Little Big Horn, Custer was widely considered the most daring and courageous cavalry officer in the Army." He was a glory hunter and was appropriately called, Squaw Killer by Native Americans. This feature glorifies Custer and leaves the student with that impression.
[Reply]:-P.198(2) Based on the reviewer's criticism, page 199 will be revised to present Indian point of view equally. Before the first paragraph, these sentences will be inserted: "Custer held quite a different reputation among Indians. He was known as 'Squaw Killer,' a man who killed just for glory."[74]

In response to Broader Perspectives' suggestion, Ginn Publishing Company agreed to consider replacing the word "fierce"[75] while the Merrill company agreed to change the phrase "working women" to "employed women"[76] in its text upon request from the Texas Education Agency. Still, one editor described decisions to correct typos and other errors with a tone of nonchalance. "Once in a while, if it was something factual that they caught us on, we would fix it, and thank them for pointing it out," she said. Similarly, Cheryl Jacobs told me,

> There's very little good photography in textbooks. The photography is really boring. You know, it might be in four color but why would you look at it? It has one Caucasian, one Hispanic, one Black, one White, and they set it up because that doesn't occur naturally too many times a day. So the spontaneity goes out of the photograph. You know we had to remove a picture in Texas (I think it was) because we had no pictures in our group's chapter on women leaders. So I guess it was a legitimate complaint, you know, so we changed the picture. I mean, sometimes it's hard to argue.

Corroborating these impressions, Dean Lindstrom, director of social studies for a publishing company, explained, "So each item falls into different categories. If something is said to be referenced for a future publication, chances are 50/50 it might make it."

While the state requires revisions in textbooks recommended for adoption, it is more likely to be concerned with factual errors than substantive ones. A factual error is "a verified error or any error that would interfere with student learning. The context, including the intended student audience and grade level appropriateness, shall be considered."[77] An examination of the Texas Education Agency's "Report of the Commissioner of Education Concerning Recommended Changes and Corrections in Textbooks" indicates that the vast majority of changes and corrections pertain to typographical errors, errors in spelling or grammar, the addition or deletion of words or brief phrases, errors in information that are unlikely to be disputed, or information needed to update a book. These changes do not extend above and beyond what most publishers agreed to do on their own.[78]

That changes in terminology are small and relatively easy to make does not mean they are necessarily insignificant in meaning. Though trivial from a practical standpoint, some of these changes do have implications for the messages in the text and this is, of course, why petitioners make their claims. What publishers' responses tell us, however, is that they did not *think about* these changes in textbook content as changes in meaning or perspective. They were primarily concerned with whether they could make the revisions readily and inexpensively. Some modifications were simply annoying, but others could be expensive if they involved rewriting paragraphs, pages, or entire chapters. The latter, publishers argued, were quite costly especially if they necessitated new versions of not only the pupil's book but also the teacher's edition and supplementary materials.

At issue was not the effect of textbook revisions on how knowledge would be interpreted or on the intended message of the book, but rather, whether revisions would be costly from an economic standpoint. Post-production changes, according to curriculum director David Caine, did not necessarily address the kinds of issues over which cultural battles are fought.

> I wouldn't say [the changes] are substantive. No, they're usually details, certainly they're typos. . . . But I can't think of a case where, now, some people say those are substantive changes, especially the special interest groups when they see that we're going to remove this picture and put in another, or we're going to change this paragraph. But I think you and I would agree that they're not substantive changes. They don't change the vision or the focus of the book. They don't change the overall message of the book.

In spite of the efforts of interested parties to contest textbook knowledge, the organization and practices of the statewide adoption system have structured the ways and extent to which their input can affect textbook selection and content. Because those employed at the Texas Education Agency largely share the professional backgrounds and interests of the textbook committee, the process has been geared to a logic that reflects educators' approach to knowledge. The following chapter explains how and why decision makers' interests have differed from those of petitioners, how the dominance of professional and commercial interests precluded attention to the cultural politics of textbook battles, and the implications of these interests for evaluating and transforming textbook knowledge.

## NOTES

Portions of this chapter, specifically pp. 25–81, appear in one of my earlier articles—"Evaluating the Content of Textbooks: Public Interests and Professional Authority," *Sociology of Education* 64 (January 1991): 11–18.

1. Carolyn Galloway, Texas Education Agency, *Transcript of Proceedings before Commissioner of Education and the State Textbook Committee*, Austin, Texas, 1985, 57.

2. Interview with state textbook committee member, October 29, 1987.

3. Gary B. Nash, Charlotte Crabtree, and Ross E. Dunn, *History on Trial: Culture Wars and the Teaching of the Past* (New York: Knopf, 1997), 43.

4. Apple, *Official Knowledge*, 44–63.

5. This event is described in Todd Gitlin's *The Twilight of Common Dreams: Why America Is Wracked by Culture Wars* (New York: Metropolitan, 1995), and prompted his analysis of the impact of identity politics on the solidarity of the Left.

6. For analyses of temperance crusades, see Joseph Gusfield, *Symbolic Crusade* (Urbana: University of Illinois Press, 1963); and for antipornography campaigns, see Louis A. Zurcher and R. George Kilpatrick, *Citizens for Decency: Antipornography Crusades as Status Defense* (Austin: University of Texas Press, 1976).

7. Ann L. Page and Donald A. Clelland, "The Kanawha County Textbook Controversy: A Study of the Politics of Life Style Concern." *Social Forces* 57 (September 1978): 1.

8. The process was officially established in the state's Reconstruction Constitution. Protesters became formally involved in the early 1960s.

9. According to chapter 66 of the Texas Administrative Code, numerous revisions to the process were made as of September 1, 1996. See Texas Administrative Code, Chapter 66. State Adoption and Distribution of Instructional Materials, Subchapter A. General Provisions www.tea.state.tx.us/rules/tac/chapter066/ch066b.html. The following include the changes since 1996 that are most pertinent to this study: (1) the state board of education issues the proclamation twenty-four months before the scheduled adoption of new materials; (2) the State Textbook Committee has been reorganized into "State Review Panels," and the commissioner of education has the authority to decide how many panels will be used in a given year, how many people will serve on each, and how the panels will be selected; (3) petitioners appear before the state board of education at public hearings; (4) publishers can be penalized for failing to correct factual errors; (5) "The Texas Education Code, Chapter 31, provides for adoption of two separate lists of instructional materials. The 'conforming' list is to consist of instructional materials that meet manufacturing standards adopted by the SBOE, contain material covering each element of essential knowledge and skills, and are free of factual errors. The 'nonconforming' list is to

consist of instructional materials submitted that meet manufacturing standards adopted by the SBOE, contain material covering at least half, but not all, of the elements of essential knowledge and skills, and are free of factual errors. Both conforming and nonconforming adopted instructional materials may be purchased by the state for school districts and open-enrollment charter schools." See Texas Education Agency Division of Textbook Administration, "Overview Textbook Adoption and Distribution," www.tea.state.tx.us/Textbooks/adoptprocess/overview.htm.

10. Staffed by about one thousand people, the Texas Education Agency in Austin certifies the state's teachers and plans the curriculum frameworks for all subject areas. I examined the 1985 and 1986 editions of the commissioner's report.

11. Prior to 1987, the committee recommended two to five books plus alternates for each subject area. In 1987, the state board increased the maximum number of books permitted to eight per subject. Because committees were allowed, but not obligated, to list as many as eight books, competition among publishers remained stiff.

12. Ada Ferguson, Texas Education Agency, *Transcript of Proceedings*, July 1985, 26.

13. McGraw-Hill Book Company, *Guidelines for Equal Treatment of the Sexes in McGraw-Hill Book Company Publications* (McGraw-Hill Book Company, New York, 1974, mimeographed), 2, 3.

14. Holt, Rinehart and Winston School Department, *Guidelines for the Development of Elementary and Secondary Instructional Materials: The Treatment of Sex Roles* (Holt, Rinehart and Winston, 1975); and McGraw-Hill, *Guidelines for Equal Treatment*, 4.

15. See Frank Piasecki, "Norma and Mel Gabler: The Development and Causes of Their Involvement Concerning the Curricular Appropriateness of School Textbook Content" (Ph.D. diss., North Texas State University, 1982), 257.

16. See Frances FitzGerald, *America Revised* (Boston: Little, Brown, 1979) for an account of various changes in school textbooks over time.

17. Referring to the index of one text, the Gablers wrote, "1) Note how many pages are listed for blacks compared to 'Indians, American: poverty and, 304–306,' 'Mexican Americans, 298–301,' 'Puerto Ricans, 291–294.' No mention of just plain 'Americans.' " Texas Education Agency, *Bills of Particulars, 1972 Adoption*, 147.

18. The Gablers on Allyn and Bacon's text, Texas Education Agency, *Bills of Particulars, 1972 Adoption*, 164.

19. Randy Hays on Holt Rinehart and Winston's text, Texas Education Agency, *Bills of Particulars, 1972 Adoption*, 2.

20. Rand McNally's answer to Beverly Hennig, Texas Education Agency, publishers' answers to the *Bills of Particulars, 1972 Adoption*, 142.

21. The Gablers on Science Research Associate's text, Texas Education Agency, *Bills of Particulars, 1972 Adoption*, 188. Regarding the same textbook, the Gablers also wrote: "Only a willfully blind person could travel foreign countries without realizing that Americans have more freedom, and even the most poverty stricken class of individuals in the U.S. are better off materially than the average middle class citizen of most other nations. This can easily be verified by anyone who has spent

time in other nations, such as students, newsmen, visiting travelers, foreigners who have moved here, etc. We can attest to this ourselves" (The Gablers, Texas Education Agency, *Bills of Particulars, 1972 Adoption*, 178).

22. Kenneth T. Jackson and Barbara B. Jackson, "Why the Time is Right to Reform the History Curriculum," in *Historical Literacy,* ed. Paul Gagnon and the Bradley Commission on History in the Schools (Boston: Houghton Mifflin, 1989), 5.

23. Jackson and Jackson, "Why the Time is Right," 7.

24. The Gablers, Texas Education Agency, *Bills of Particulars, 1972 Adoption*, 189.

25. The Gablers, Texas Education Agency, *Bills of Particulars, 1972 Adoption*, 265.

26. These women's groups submitted a large portion of the testimony and bills presented to the state from 1973 to 1979.

27. See Allyn and Bacon's reply to Janie Hickie, Texas Women's Political Caucus, Texas Education Agency, *Publishers' Answers to the Bills of Particulars, 1972 Adoption*, 62.

28. Cathy Bonner, Texas Women's Political Caucus, Texas Education Agency, *Transcript of Proceedings*, textbook hearings, September 1972, 3–134.

29. Janie Hickie on Field Educational Publication's text, Texas Education Agency, *Bills of Particulars, 1972 Adoption*, 108.

30. Interview by author with Marjorie Randal, Texas NOW Bay Area chapter, April 20, 1988.

31. Prior to 1984, petitioners' testimony was limited to negative commentary so that positive input could not be used to favor particular publishers. However, in 1984, People for the American Way (PFAW) successfully lobbied the state legislature to remove the restriction against positive comments. The group's primary aim was to counter the claims of predominantly conservative interests who were allegedly seeking to censor textbooks. The removal of the restriction made it possible for petitioners to defend as well as critique textbooks. Broader Perspectives provided such appraisals.

32. Texas Education Agency, *Written Comments, 1985 Adoption*, 469.

33. Texas Education Agency, *Written Comments, 1985 Adoption*, 643.

34. Texas Education Agency, *Written Comments, 1985 Adoption*, 644.

35. Texas Education Agency, *Written Comments, 1985 Adoption*, 670.

36. Texas Education Agency, *Written Comments, 1985 Adoption*, 649.

37. Texas Education Agency, *Written Comments, 1985 Adoption*, 662.

38. Texas Education Agency, *Written Comments, 1985 Adoption*, 669.

39. Texas Education Agency, *Written Comments, 1985 Adoption*, 680.

40. Billy C. Hutcheson, Texas State Daughters of the American Revolution (TSDAR) in *Report to TSDAR*, March 1986. Photocopy.

41. Based in Washington, D.C., PFAW also provided legal defense for school districts in Alabama and Tennessee where ultraconservative parents attempted to ban certain textbooks from use.

42. PFAW, *Looking at History* (Washington, D.C.: People for the American Way, 1985), 180.

43. PFAW, *Looking at History*, 187.

44. Dr. Isabel Pritchard, on behalf of NOW, in Texas Education Agency, *Transcript of Proceedings, 1979 Adoption*, 27.

45. Interview by author with Rema Lou Brown, Texas chapter of NOW, May 2, 1988.

46. Broader Perspectives, Texas Education Agency, *Written Comments, 1985 Adoption*, 468.

47. PFAW, *We the People* (Washington, D.C.: People for the American Way, 1987), iv, also 9. One reviewer described a dry textbook activity that called "for students to 'research the judicial branch of government and prepare an outline on the findings.' "

48. PFAW, *We the People*, viii.

49. Douglas Yates, *Bureaucratic Democracy* (Cambridge, Mass.: Harvard University Press, 1982).

50. See Yates, *Bureaucratic Democracy.*

51. The following example illustrates the problem of attributing decisions about textbook selection to a particular petitioner's input. To assess a petitioner's influence on the adoption or rejection of a book, we might compare the petitioner's testimony and/or written comments to how the textbook committee votes. If the testimony was negative and the committee rejected the textbook in question, we might infer that there is a relationship between the petitioner's protests and the committee's action. However, because textbooks typically contain both strengths and weaknesses, petitioners usually do not reject or support books in their entirety. More frequently, they object to specific statements and sections in a book. Rather than saying, "I approve of textbook A; I don't approve of textbook B," they are more likely to say, "I prefer this part of book A; I reject this part of book A. I approve this part of book B, I reject." They may prefer the treatment of Martin Luther King in one text, but criticize its portrayal of Eleanor Roosevelt. Since publishers often provide very similar texts, each is likely to be the focus of some complaints. Often petitioners will make the same comments about several or all of the books up for adoption in a subject category.

Finally, it is common for groups that support different ideologies to object to features in the same books. Thus, it is difficult to determine which ideological pressures might have influenced the books selected or rejected. For example, in the 1985 adoption of high school U.S. history textbooks, the Texas textbook committee recommended books by the following publishers: Scott Foresman, Harcourt Brace Jovanovich, Coronado, Ginn, and Houghton Mifflin. Table 3 indicates the preferences of three petitioning organizations, the Gablers' Educational Research Analysts, PFAW, and Broader Perspectives.

As table 3 indicates, none of the groups shared all of the preferences of the textbook committee. PFAW and Broader Perspectives, whose interests are primarily progressive, shared only one choice in common. Yet each supported two books preferred by Educational Research Analysts, whose concerns reflect traditionalist interests. Hence, even if textbook committees acknowledged the effects of advocacy groups, which they usually do not, the direct impact of particular groups would be almost impossible to discern.

52. Kenneth K. Wong and Tom Loveless, "The Politics of Textbook Policy: Proposing a Framework," in *Textbooks in American Society*, ed. Philip G. Altbach, Gail P. Kelly, Hugh G. Petrie, and Lois Weis (Albany, N.Y.: SUNY Press, 1991), 28.

**Table 3   U.S. History Textbook Preferences, 1985 Adoption**

| *Textbook Committee* | *Educational Research Analysts* |
|---|---|
| Scott Foresman | Scribner (1) |
| Harcourt Brace Jovanovich | Scribner (2) |
| Coronado | Merrill |
| Ginn | McDougal Littell |
| Houghton Mifflin | Houghton Mifflin |

| *People For the American Way* | *Broader Perspectives* |
|---|---|
| Ginn | Scott Foresman |
| Harcourt Brace Jovanovich | Scribner (2) |
| Holt, Rinehart, Winston | Addison-Wesley |
| McDougal, Littell | McDougal, Littell |
| Houghton Mifflin | Prentice-Hall |

*Note:* In 1985, Scribner offered two different textbooks, (1) *A History of the American Nation from 1877*, and (2) *Heritage of Freedom from 1877*.

53. Wong and Loveless, "The Politics of Textbook Policy," 37.

54. Before 1985 and since 1989, Texas citizens have elected members of the state board of education to represent each of twenty-seven congressional districts. An appointed board, selected during former Governor Mark White's term, served from 1985 to 1989.

55. During the period of study, the Texas State Textbook Committee was a body of classroom teachers, administrators, and curriculum specialists nominated by their school districts and appointed by the state board of education to serve in the annual textbook selection process. In selecting members, the state sought to achieve geographical diversity as well as a range of educational expertise and experience. For example, of 104 textbook committee members who served on 7 different adoption committees between 1969 and 1986, 62 were classroom teachers; 21 were directors, supervisors, or coordinators of curricular programs or departments; 14 were superintendents or deputy superintendents; 4 were counselors; and 3 were principals.

56. The sample included the following: 10 men and 19 women; 9 curriculum supervisors, 14 classroom teachers, 2 principals, 3 superintendents, and 1 counselor. Twenty-three members were white, five were black, and one, Hispanic. The years in which committee members served and the number of members in each year is as follows: (1) 1966, (3) 1969, (4) 1972, (6) 1978, (3) 1979, (1) 1982, (7) 1985, and (4) 1986. The members represented the following locations: (6) Houston area, (3) Austin area, (2) San Antonio, (3) Amarillo, (2) Midland, (3) Fort Worth/Dallas, (3) Gulf Coast, and (1) Harlingen, Abilene, Waxahachie, Cooper, Temple, Longview, San Angelo. I interviewed textbook committee members by phone, in their homes, or at their places of employment. I have changed the names of all interviewees. In quoted material, I use ellipses to indicate information deleted because it was not essential to understanding what was said.

57. Alvin Gouldner, *The Dialectic of Ideology and Technology* (New York: Oxford University Press, 1982), 246.

58. Gouldner, *Dialectic of Ideology*, 264.

59. The interviews were conducted by phone or in person with nine publishing representatives from seven different publishing houses that had or were publishing textbooks for sale in Texas. Their positions were as follows: two directors of social studies, one national sales manager, one southwestern regional vice president, one national consultant and former sales representative, three executive editors of social studies, and one vice president and curriculum director. The length of interviews ranged from one-half hour to ninety minutes. The names of publishing representatives have been changed. In quoted material, I use ellipses to indicate information deleted because it was not essential to understanding what was said.

60. See Arnie Weissman, "Building the Tower of Babel," *Texas Outlook* (Winter 1981–82): 10–15 and 29–33.

61. In some cases publishers responded by offering a counterargument and citing sources to defend their material. In other instances they agreed to make changes or corrections, though they were not obligated to add, delete, or revise material unless the Texas Education Agency or state board made adoption contingent on specific changes.

62. Allyn and Bacon's response to the Gablers, Texas Education Agency, *Publishers' Answers to Bills of Particulars, 1972 Adoption*, 88.

63. Harcourt Brace Jovanovich's response to Mr. and Mrs. Carl S. Droste and Mr. and Mrs. Earnest Barcuch, Texas Education Agency, *Publishers' Answers to Bills of Particulars, 1978 Adoption*, 18.

64. Allyn and Bacon's response to the Gablers, Texas Education Agency, *Publishers' Answers to Bills of Particulars, 1978 Adoption*, 69.

65. Allyn and Bacon, Texas Education Agency, *Publishers' Answers to Bills of Particulars, 1978 Adoption*, 70.

66. Allyn and Bacon, Texas Education Agency, *Publishers' Answers to Bills of Particulars, 1978 Adoption*, 67.

67. Laidlaw's response to Janie Hickie, Texas Education Agency, *Publishers' Answers to Bills of Particulars, 1972 Adoption*, 1.

68. Laidlaw, Texas Education Agency, *Publishers' Answers to Bills of Particulars, 1972 Adoption*, 2.

69. E. D. Hirsch Jr., *Cultural Literacy* (Boston: Houghton Mifflin, 1987), 106.

70. Rand McNally's response to Ms. Suzanne Gott, Texas Women's Political Caucus, Texas Education Agency, *Publishers' Answers to Bills of Particulars, 1972 Adoption*, 20.

71. Myra Sadker and David Sadker, *Failing at Fairness* (New York: Touchstone, 1994), 72.

72. Scribner's response to the Gablers, Texas Education Agency, *Responses to Written Comments, 1985 Adoption*, 847.

73. Coronado's response to Broader Perspectives, Texas Education Agency, *Responses to Written Comments, 1985 Adoption*, 221.

74. Coronado's response to Broader Perspectives, Texas Education Agency, *Responses to Written Comments, 1985 Adoption*, 235.

75. Ginn's response to Broader Perspectives, Texas Education Agency, *Responses to Written Comments, 1985 Adoption*, 277.

76. Merrill's response to Broader Perspectives, Texas Education Agency, *Responses to Written Comments, 1985 Adoption*, 687.

77. See Texas Education Code, Chapter 66. State Adoption and Distribution of Instructional Materials. Subchapter A. General Provisions. 66.10. Procedures Governing Violations of Statutes—Administration Penalties at www.tea.state.tx.us/rules/tac/chapter066/ch066a.html.

78. In 1986, petitioner Steven Schafersman of the Texas Council for Science Education criticized the process of correcting textbooks at a November meeting of the state board of education. He reported: "Of the four earth science books that I would keep on the adoption list, only the one by Silver Burdett needs no scientific revision. The book by Merrill has an inaccurate discussion of the principle of uniformitarianism that should have been revised by the TEA staff, but wasn't. The book by MacMillan has a one-sentence description of evolution that needed to be expanded, but the staff did not require this. The book by Addison-Wesley misrepresents evolution in a number of ways, but the section was not revised by the textbook staff. . . . All publishers were willing to make any legitimate changes requested by the TEA staff, but the scientifically advantageous changes I pointed out were not requested. These problems may seem minor to you, but they reflect considerably on the integrity of science education in Texas. I repeat: you are being ill-served by your staff. (Texas Education Agency, *Proceedings before the State Board of Education*, November, 1986, taped recording by Texas Education Agency.)

## 3

# Choosing School Knowledge: Textbook Selection in Texas

If the system of textbook adoption relegates the cultural politics of text-book battles to the realm of interest group opinion and philosophy, by what criteria *is* textbook knowledge selected and produced? This chapter shows how decisions about knowledge are shaped by professional norms, commercial imperatives, and the institutional contexts in which decisions are made. Textbook selection committees, while not entirely dismissive of issues such as accuracy and meaning, are concerned primarily with how schoolbooks can be used to organize classroom lessons and to facilitate students' *acquisition* of knowledge. In turn, educators' needs and opinions affect publishers' behaviors and the latter's interest in including new and different knowledges.

The notion of acquisition is significant because it suggests a way of thinking about the purpose of knowledge that is very different from the cultural concerns at the heart of public mobilizations. The criteria with which books are judged and the technocratic logic and procedures by which key actors make decisions reflect rational-purposive objectives that limit a critical evaluation of textbook knowledge as well as the potential for implementing radical changes in educational content. Ultimately, textbook selection committees and publishers are more likely to contribute to the recontextualization of knowledge than to its reconstruction or transformation.

## PRAGMATIC DECISIONS

When textbook committees convened to choose books in August, a two-thirds majority vote was required to place a book on their list of recommendations. In most years examined, committees opted to vote

49

without discussion and to entertain comments and opinions from one another only when they did not obtain a majority vote on the first ballot. So, unless a second or third ballot was needed, we learned little about what factors determined their choices. In three out of six adoptions for secondary-level U.S. history and government books, the committee selected five books on the first ballot.

However, in 1985 the selection of U.S. history texts required ten ballots. Discussions between ballots provided insight into what the committee members' book evaluations are based on and how they determined, as one put it, "what the state wanted." Listening to conversations among the committee members, I found that they and their advisors were highly interested in and impressed by the physical and pedagogical characteristics of textbooks.[1] These features included readability, versatility, organization, length of chapters, vocabulary skills, coverage of topics, quality of graphs, charts, writing style and illustrations, and the inclusion of time lines, introductory outlines, and end-of-chapter questions. Occasionally, discussants mentioned specific topics in American history such as Watergate and the balanced treatment of ethnic groups; yet, they noted these substantive facets of textbooks far less frequently than features related to appearance and usability. Moreover, when committees referred to the presence or absence of historical events in textbooks, they usually did not discuss their treatment—whether coverage was comprehensive or one-sided, cynical or idealistic—in great depth.

**Table 4  Number of Ballots Required**

| Year | High School U.S. History | | |
| | Number of Books Offered | Number Recommended | Number of Ballots |
| --- | --- | --- | --- |
| 1972 | 12 | 5 | 1 |
| 1978* | 7 | 5 | 1 |
| 1985 | 13 | 5 | 10 |

| Year | High School Civil Government | | |
| | Number of Books Offered | Number Recommended | Number of Ballots |
| --- | --- | --- | --- |
| 1972 | 13 | 5 | 4 |
| 1979** | 10 | 5 | 4 |
| 1986 | 7 | 5 | 1 |

*The committee recommended one alternate textbook.
**The committee recommended two alternate textbooks.

By focusing on the instructional aspects of textbooks, committee members felt they were evaluating textbook knowledge as they were supposed to, or as one person put it, according to what was important "education-wise." How a textbook might appeal to students with different abilities and how well it would provide the skills and information tested on statewide exams were among the highest priorities. Relating how she defined and assessed the content of a book, math teacher and former committee member Katherine Smith asked herself:

> Is this something you can teach? Is it something the children will understand? . . . are the explanations good? . . . Is it a book that is adaptable to a child who is struggling with his subject? Does it give you a chance as a teacher to branch out and challenge those who are adept in a subject?

Studies of textbook evaluation practices confirm that graphics and instructional aspects of textbooks are a central part of evaluation instruments employed at state and local levels of adoption.[2] Content per se receives significantly less notice. According to one author, evaluators' priorities reflect two related assumptions, that subject–area authorities write textbooks (and thus will naturally provide accurate information), and that selection committees lack sufficient expertise to judge the quality and accuracy of material covered. [3]

Some committee members agreed with these assumptions. They felt confident about the credibility and judgment of textbook authors and they thought they were personally unqualified to question an author's selection and presentation of knowledge. Nor did they wish to take responsibility for making editorial revisions or correcting typographical errors. Susan Johnson, a school curriculum supervisor of social studies, described how she assessed her duties:

> Is the role of the textbook person an editor who edits these books for errors in content, inaccuracies, and that kind of thing? Or are we there also to look at the instructional quality of that program, in other words the kind of learning activities that accompany the program?

## ALTERNATIVE NOTIONS
## OF DIVERSITY

Committees must and did take into account not simply their own preferences, but also the needs of students and teachers in school districts all over the state. In some instances, decisions came down to a basic need

to ensure that schools would have some kind of textbook in their classrooms by the start of the next academic year. For courses in relatively
new subjects, evaluators had little choice but to adopt books despite
their deficiencies. Betty Sue Taylor, a teacher from Temple, Texas, said,
"I recall that some of the committee did not feel that any of the books
in one category were very meritorious, yet we tried to pick the best of
what was offered." The explanations other committee members offered
for their behaviors gave added meaning to what the concept of diversity
means in state-level decision making. Peter Quinn, a deputy superintendent of curriculum, explained:

> I argued for a book that personally, my educational philosophy thinks is the
> wrong way to approach the teaching of reading. And yet I knew that the
> approach was so different that somewhere in this state there were probably
> some schools that really needed that approach because what they had been
> doing in the past does not work with their population, and I argued very hard
> for it, and got it because I felt that it should have been one of the options.

In making such decisions evaluators asked themselves if students
would be able to read the books; whether textbook content provided a
stimulating intellectual experience was another matter and sometimes
an irrelevant one. In contrast to the kinds of issues more likely to be of
interest to academic scholars, textbook committees stressed the importance of accessible information. They were not at all embarrassed to say
they considered the lowest levels of student ability when evaluating a
book's potential usefulness. On the contrary, they felt obligated to do
so. Ann Simmons, a high school English teacher, observed:

> On the quality of writing, most critics don't realize that when you're choosing
> for an entire state, you have to consider the border towns, the inner city areas
> of Houston and Dallas, the rural areas—we have to think in different terms
> from those with master's or Ph.D.'s who want a good history book to read.

As professionals, committees sought to accommodate the interests of
diverse populations regardless of their own ideological or pedagogical
preferences. Yet in these instances, diversity referred to level of student
preparation rather than issues of race, ethnicity, culture, or class. Certainly there are likely connections between these variables; indeed, later
multicultural reforms would be based on assumptions about these rela-
tionships. However, the committee members I interviewed did not
make or explicitly recognize these connections. I did not hear claims
that students' interests or abilities might be enhanced by making textbook material culturally relevant. These educators were keenly aware

of students' differences, but they did not attribute much significance to those differences unless they were evaluating books in an area in which ethnic differences had obvious implications, such as a reader for bilingual students.

Again, regardless of their own positions, committees tended to refrain from mandating what should be taught. In 1986, the state textbook committee recommended five health textbooks, including one that did not cover the topic of human reproduction. While most members had ranked this particular textbook lower than their preferred choices, they sought to offer local districts a range of options. In November, the committee's chairperson informed the state board of education, "I do not believe it is the responsibility of the state to dictate to 1,100 school districts the extent to which they teach sex education."[4]

## HOW THE STATE DEFINES KNOWLEDGE

To further explain their choices former members of the state's textbook committee emphasized their close adherence to state mandates and procedures. The criteria with which they evaluated schoolbooks were based on not only their own teaching experiences, but also on guidelines from the state. The state's conception of knowledge is reflected in how it structures textbook evaluation. Leona Warwick, a district English department director, who served in 1985, recalled:

> They're [the advisors] not encouraged to look at books in terms of content, and then write it up. The forms that come from the state are about mechanical changes, rather than content-related. The state gives a certain number of forms to committee members and we just pass them on. That form may influence what's done and what's not done.

State guidelines for textbook content also affect what committees look for in books and how they view the knowledge they are evaluating. Developed by the Texas Education Agency, a 1970s curricular policy called "Framework for the Social Studies" and the "essential elements," which were put in place in 1985, exercised a strong influence on the evaluation process. The "essential elements" listed in outline form topics, events, and activities texts must include. Although some interviewees felt these guidelines helped to structure and standardize evaluation as intended, they also acknowledged that the elements motivated committees to evaluate books according to whether they contained information or skills, but not necessarily with respect to how they presented knowledge. The elements basically provided a quick-step method by which publishers could show they had met state requirements and committees could verify that they had done so. John Brady, who taught government, said:

> We are bound by the essential elements. We have to teach them. . . . These favor educational objectives. They are so loosely written that the textbook writers have taken those Essential Elements and made them fit what they're writing. They have gone to the extent of printing out where each element is, where each sub-element is in the book. But it is easier for local textbook committees and the state textbook committee to select books because it diminishes the influence of petitioners.

Stressing how the elements addressed pedagogical rather than substantive concerns, Quinn observed, "No one is saying our kids need to be more conscious of citizenship and the textbooks are a way into that. You know, we're talking about essential elements. They're vague and ambiguous and basic-skill oriented."

State prescriptions restricted the committee's capacity to evaluate and affect educational content as well as teachers' capacity to be innovative in their classrooms. Smith asserted that the essential elements imposed too much structure on classroom practice. Because the state requires students to master certain skills for standardized exams, teachers felt compelled to follow rigid lesson plans. She described her frustrations with state requirements this way:

> [They are] good and bad. I think they are very very good in that they are requiring that every student have these things taught to them. But I resent them tremendously because it locks me in, and I do not have the flexibility that I once had to do what I feel like.

In spite of these reservations, most members treated the essential elements as a primary means of assessing textbook content and none elaborated on what kinds of criteria they would use if they had the freedom and flexibility to do as they pleased. Instead, if the material and objectives included in a text could be correlated with the elements, the text satisfied the state's requirement for content. Additionally, clear objectives, exercises, and instructional aids were important because they provided strategies for classroom management.

In sum, committee members focused on technical and pragmatic concerns for several reasons. First, textbook features that pertained to classroom practice make up a major part of the evaluation guidelines they received from the state and from local districts. Second, state mandates specified what topics must be included, but not how they should be treated. Third, as noted in chapter 2, committees did not view decisions about substantive or philosophical matters as part of their professional responsibility, and they were not encouraged to evaluate knowledge in more substantive ways.

## EMPOWERED INTELLECTUALS OR TECHNICIANS OF THE STATE?

Although decision makers' behaviors can be readily explained, we cannot overlook their implications for teachers' autonomy, for their participation in progressive change, and for theoretical visions of educational transformation. Radical progressive theories envision teachers as intellectuals who participate in a discourse of "critique and possibility."[5] According to this view, teachers "must take active responsibility for raising serious questions about what they teach, how they are to teach it, and what the larger goals are for which they are striving."[6] However, educators' tasks and how they conceive of them are, in fact, consistent more with a "logic of technical control" than with effective participation in critical discourse and social change.[7] When the kinds of questions that drive curricular battles become secondary to accumulating decontextualized, atomistic facts and mastering standardized tests, teachers lose the capacity to select what knowledge is taught and how; as theorists Stanley Aronowitz and Henry Giroux posit, they become little more than technicians of the state.

> One consequence is that decisions and questions over what counts as knowledge, what is worth teaching, how one judges the purpose and nature of instruction, how one views the role of school in society, and what the latter implies for understanding how specific social and cultural interests shape all levels of school life, is removed from the collective influence of teachers themselves.[8]

The effort to separate textbook evaluation from the meanings and values inherent in school knowledge disempowers teachers and reflects a false assumption about the objectivity of knowledge. The nature of their role in textbook evaluation can be viewed as part of a broader trend in educational practice whereby teachers experience diminished control over their own work.[9]

Thus, while some committee members believed they lacked the

expertise to critically evaluate content per se, according to the above argument, limited expertise is in part a product of de-skilling. As state officials and experts outside of the classroom decide what counts as knowledge, educators lose their claims to expertise. Because knowledge is conceptualized as "essential elements," that is, packaged, presented, received, and tested as discrete facts, and detached from social, historical, or political meanings, it appears to be unquestionable. As Giroux put it, "Questions concerning the social construction of knowledge and the constitutive interests behind the selection, organization, and evaluation of 'brute facts' are buried under the assumption that knowledge is objective and value free."[10] The formulation of educational knowledge as "elements" creates a sense of givenness that shapes how teachers evaluate and use textbooks.

Consequently, teachers were unlikely to contest dominant narratives because they did not see official knowledge as knowledge about women, civil rights, and diversity or as knowledge that could be presented from different perspectives. The "interrogation of the content itself" and the examination of ideological representations,[11] tasks that are central to radical progressive agendas, cannot be performed once knowledge becomes "divorced from the political and cultural traditions that give it meaning."[12]

> In essence, questions of "why" are transformed into questions of "how to." The result of this, combined with the fact that serious conflict is usually absent from the curriculum itself, is that the instrumental ideologies replace ethical and political awareness and debate.[13]

Because the processes through which knowledge is selected are expedient and regulated externally, they do not facilitate the kinds of discussions that make alternative curricular constructions possible. On the contrary, the social construction of knowledge and how it is mandated, packaged, and taught are rendered invisible.[14]

## INSTITUTIONAL STRUCTURES AND EDUCATIONAL DECISION MAKING

Why textbook committees spent little time discussing whose knowledge is being taught was a function not only of how knowledge is conceived, but also of the institutional context in which decisions about knowledge were made. In addition to prescribing evaluation criteria, the organization of textbook selection structured what committee members were able to accomplish. As described in chapter 2, committee members performed many tasks within a strictly timed schedule. They organized subgroups of advisors and met with publishing representatives; they were presented with volumes of petitioners' comments. In a single adoption year, a committee might deal with as many as one hundred texts designed for multiple subject areas.

When members met to choose a list of books, they could, in theory, deliberate about particular textbooks as long as they wished and cast as many ballots as necessary. In reality, the schedule and process of collective decision making limited the topics and dynamics of committee discussion. Because committees were required to vote on a large number of books in a short period they lacked the time and the stamina to engage in lengthy discussion of specific issues. I sensed an unspoken norm that discouraged prolonged debate and numerous ballots. Concerned about delaying the process, committee members were reticent, if not apologetic, about offering opinions or extending deliberations. They often hesitated, as if to say, "I don't mean to open a can of worms, but my advisors said . . ."

While time constraints precluded serious attention to how textbooks present knowledge, even if time had been available, no guidelines existed to address these matters. The adoption process prescribed general objectives, a division of duties, and a scheduling of tasks, but it was not set up to pay close attention to textbook ideas and messages. Because members had little knowledge of what issues would arise in their meeting and whether they would need to defend a textbook preference or on what grounds, they made decisions as choice opportunities presented themselves. In this sense, the committee's procedures conformed to a garbage-can style of decision making, an ad hoc process through which content-related issues, when addressed at all, were raised without plan or predictability and thus escaped full attention.[15]

The consistency of petitioners' objections from cycle to cycle attests to how a focus on specific substantive matters might be short-lived even when given. Since the state adopts textbooks for different subjects each year, the evaluation of textbook knowledge in a particular area begins anew in each cycle. Also, replacing committees each year creates a flow of participants and provides a weak information base with few lessons from previous adoptions.[16] Consequently, whether committee members initiated discussion usually depended not on a collective agenda but on the will and assertiveness of particular individuals. Those who were better prepared and more willing to discuss textbook material in detail were more likely to voice their opinions and to affect the views of their colleagues. For example, one member, who represented a school district with ample resources and support, persuaded less-informed colleagues to agree with her choices. Laura Jarvis acknowledged:

> I was able to sway the votes on several books because I was dealing with the facts. There are some members who don't speak and don't have an opinion. They are not in a strong position to negotiate for educational excellence. They vote as their advisors tell them. [Because] the system is insistent on drawing from such a broad political base, they don't have the skills to analyze in terms of whether the books are appropriate.

In contrast to Jarvis's confidence, for the average committee member, the state process was an eye-opener. Carolyn Craft, a classroom teacher in health education, described the disadvantages of being a newcomer to the process.

> There is a problem with the TEA set up. The committee members are not given good enough orientation about what to expect. They have no idea of the pitfalls. They don't really know what they are doing until it's too late. And you never get to repeat it. We suggested there should be a member pulled from the previous committee each year to tell what is needed, [what are] some of the pitfalls. It would help to get some consistency. Now some people deviated from the forms [lists of criteria]. Those with experience, like some administrators, had some background with textbook adoption. They were aware of who the publishers were and what was involved, what to expect. [We] peons who were classroom teachers didn't have that.

Instead of perceiving the process as an opportunity to talk about content, most committee members were more likely to ask, "What do I do?" Unlike petitioners, they did not come to the process to recommend changes or question textbook biases, nor were they positioned to do so particularly when making decisions about books in areas beyond their expertise. Craft further explained:

> It is implied that you're supposed to represent your advisors. It varies with your background. In your area of expertise you might take your advisors' votes in mind, make tradeoffs, go to look at what they liked, but then go with your own judgment. In Calculus, for example, I had to go by my advisors. I was more inclined to be swayed by members of the committee if it was not my area of expertise. My advisors were not there so I could say, 'Hey guys, what do you want?' I was more inclined to switch my vote in situations where I didn't have expertise. The specialist on the committee then has a lot of weight.

As a result, the selection committees I observed behaved conservatively and confined their tasks to designated duties rather than extending their "bounds of responsibility."[17] Some members felt they had done their job, which was not to evaluate paragraphs or prescribe values to be taught, but to come up with a list of books. Most defended their decisions against suggestions from the public or the state board that they had neglected their responsibilities or overlooked weaknesses in textbooks.[18]

And rightfully so. The particular interests and objectives of textbook selection committees should not imply that members skirted their responsibilities or expended little effort. On the contrary, I found them to be a dedicated group that put much time and energy into the selection process with minimal compensation. Nonetheless, the structure of the process was not designed to entertain the kinds of substantive concerns petitioners raised, to evaluate specific passages and recommend changes, or to consider possibilities for major revisions. The fact that there was no formal means of monitoring the consequences of committee choices and decisions limited accountability. Books recommended in August of a given year would not reach classrooms until September of the following year. By that time, the state would have already appointed a new textbook committee for the next textbook adoption.

## MAKING SENSE OF DECISION-MAKING PRACTICES

The contradictions within the process were striking. Textbook selection presumably requires professional expertise, but individuals had minimal opportunity to use their expertise to evaluate subject matter. In actuality, educators selected books for subjects in which they had little expertise and given that they could only serve on a selection committee once, they came to the process with little or no prior experience. The process of choosing members of a textbook committee contributed to a level of demographic representation that would be less attainable with a fixed body of professional elites. But just as the committee had limited opportunity to collectively affect content, individual members had virtually no autonomy to address particular needs and interests or to generate alternative ideas about what textbooks should contain and how they should be evaluated.

In light of how the procedures of the adoption process structured committee behaviors, it is important to be clear about what structure means in this case. Although processes of statewide textbook adoption appear to exercise tight control over educational knowledge, regulation pertains more to the organizational structure of textbook selection—who chooses books, when, and with what procedures—than to educational content, per se. These findings are consistent with the view that educational organizations are restricted in their capacity to monitor the actual inspection of educational knowledge.[19]

If we expect, as petitioners do, that decisions about textbook selection should involve choices about substantive content, the process of choosing textbooks does not make much sense. However, the ritualistic institutionalization of procedures does serve important functions; it creates the appearance that knowledge is being carefully chosen even though there may be little attention paid to what is actually being taught. In this way, centralized adoption systems typify the behaviors of loosely coupled educational organizations[20] that strive to meet "external definitions of structural rationality."[21] Educational systems, according to theories of loose coupling, "lack close internal coordination, especially of the content and methods of what is presumably their main activity—instruction. Instruction tends to be removed from the control of the organizational structure, in both its bureaucratic and its collegial aspects."[22] Specific goals regarding substantive issues neither inform nor motivate decisions about what is to be taught. Rather, the state, and those who serve it, participate in a process that confirms and legitimizes its role in administering education, while decoupling decision-making activities from educational outcomes.

As such, controversial decisions, policies, and practices unlikely to meet societal expectations are likely to be avoided. A form of reproduction occurs but for different reasons than those reproduction theorists suggest. Dramatic shifts in educational content are improbable, not because dominant social groups are strategically exercising ideological control over knowledge selection, but because decision makers do not pay close attention to content per se.

Thus, textbook selection appears rational in that it is governed by a predetermined schedule, a set of rules and a structure of roles and authority. Yet, the process of making choices matters more than the outcomes that are produced. Procedures, contextual norms, and technical criteria influenced the types of decisions textbook committees made and how they defined educational objectives. Meanwhile, the selection committee's detachment from controversy reinforced its professional identity. By confining their choices and decisions to the specific demands and expectations of the process, evaluators fulfilled their accommodative and organizational functions.

## TEACHERS' INTERESTS AND THE PRODUCTION OF TEXTBOOK KNOWLEDGE

Teachers' needs and interests are important not only because they affect which books are chosen for use in school classrooms, but also because they bear weight on the decisions of schoolbook publishers who play a central role in the production of school knowledge. Like educators and state officials, publishers behave in ways that are strongly influenced by their locations within particular institutional structures and systems of organization. While critics of school materials raise questions about whose knowledge is being presented and how, publishers approach decisions about knowledge through a language of commerce. As part of a large profit-making industry, editors and marketing representatives pay close attention to economic imperatives—what will sell to the greatest number of buyers, how much should be invested in a new text—that have significant consequences for whether new knowledges are incorporated in the curriculum and how issues such as diversity are managed.

Situating textbook publishing in a broader context of cultural production enables us to better understand how and why major publishing decisions also have little to do with the kinds of debates that characterize struggles over educational knowledge. Studies of editorial and marketing decisions in trade book publishing, the news industry, and television entertainment, for example, have illuminated how economic imperatives and organizational norms supercede aesthetic and intellectual concerns.[23] In his study of decision making among trade book editors, Walter Powell found that although editors are key gatekeepers who have the power to accept or reject scholarly manuscripts, long-standing organizational practices and forms of unobtrusive control limit their autonomy.[24] Similarly, Lewis Coser et al. describe how college textbook publishers hire teams of writers and researchers to prepare "managed texts," thus reducing the creative license of individual authors.[25] These studies have advanced sociological analyses of cultural production beyond deterministic theories that treat culture as a reflection of society as well as beyond equally simplistic views of artists and authors as autonomous creators and decision makers.[26] Their findings are especially relevant to schoolbook publishing.

Decision making in the production of elementary and secondary schoolbooks, known in the industry as the "el-hi" sector, is shaped significantly by what Pierre Bourdieu has termed large-scale cultural production.[27] In contrast to restricted production, through which producers seek long-run profits and "aesthetically legitimate" work,[28] large-scale cultural producers compete for economic capital and material profits by gaining control of the biggest possible market.[29] Profit-making strategies influence how producers conceive of their products. Restricted producers compete for authority through recognition, consecration, and prestige; they are more likely to focus on the aesthetic, intellectual, or artistic attributes of their products. In comparison, consumer-oriented producers are not especially concerned with these qualities. Although we might think of publishers as "prime guardians" of a nation's symbolic culture,[30] culture, defined in terms of shared meanings, values, and ideas, is not a central issue of textbook production. Rather, as Michael Apple has argued, schoolbooks are "geared to what will sell and not necessarily to what it is most important to know."[31]

> In the increasingly conglomerate-owned publishing field, censorship and ideological control as we commonly think of them are less of a problem than might be anticipated. It is not ideological conformity or some political agenda that accounts for many of the ideas that are ultimately made or not made available to the larger public. Rather, it is the infamous "bottom line" that counts.[32]

By recognizing the impact of organizational imperatives on how a product is made, a production of culture perspective appropriately contextualizes publishing decisions in ways that neither reproduction theories nor theories of counterhegemony take into account. While the former portray publishers as instruments of elite domination, the latter assume that publishers respond reflexively to pressures from social movements. In fact, neither view is complete. Whether one is for or against including new knowledges and perspectives, the culture wars do not carry much weight at the editorial desks where decisions about school knowledge are made. Although publishers care about quality, quality has less to do with ideas than combatants in debates over knowledge might expect.

But while the relationship between market demands and publishing decisions is central to understanding how textbooks are produced, it still fails to explain why textbooks take the particular form and shape that they do, and why, for example, a 1992 textbook mentioned only eleven female names despite years of advocacy from women's groups.[33] The argument that publishers focus on the bottom line, though persuasive, is useful only to the extent that we can specify the factors that define the bottom line. What matters is not merely the existence of particular markets, but how cultural producers read, interpret, and even construct their markets.[34] As one author has put it, "While culture is dependent on economic factors 'it is worth repeating that economic is not independent of the social-institutional.' "[35] In the production of school textbook knowledge, these social-institutional factors include the needs and interests of textbook selection committees and the teachers whom they represent, as well as the organizational priorities that shape publishers' decisions. A former president of Follett Publishing Company summarized the importance of textbook evaluators this way:

> Now that committees will not select programs unless they represent minorities fairly, publishers go to extreme lengths to recognize every minority group in proper proportion, no matter how much this may distort history or diminish learning. Should committees adopt books that challenge youngsters, publishers will enrich the content of their materials and write them at higher reading levels. If committees select only titles even the poorest reader can easily absorb, publishers will scramble to simplify vocabulary, shorten sentences, and use more illustrations. If committees are reluctant to choose titles that cover the theory of evolution, publishers will find ways to minimize the discussion of evolution in their textbooks. If committees show a preference for colorful illustrations, publishers will splash full-color illustrations on every page.
>
> Critics of textbooks have urged a variety of reforms upon publishers—to little effect. When the critics succeed in changing the basis on which adoption committees select textbooks, publishers will change the textbooks they publish.[36]

The editors and curriculum directors with whom I spoke affirmed this view. Their perceptions of educators' needs and preferences, not ideological conflicts and pressures, most influenced their decisions.

## RATIONALITY, UTILITY, AND CLASSROOM MANAGEMENT

The interests of textbook committees as described in this chapter affect how publishers conceive of knowledge and the kinds of books they produce. Publishers concurred that the key selling features of teachers' textbook editions include material that correlates with state content guidelines, the availability of sample tests and lesson plans, and suggested classroom strategies and student activities. Teachers' interest in usability and design feeds back to textbook publishers who then devote a great deal of attention to the style, visual appeal, and readability of their books.

We should not assume that publishers necessarily agreed with teachers' priorities. Several publishers expressed disappointment with how selection committees evaluate schoolbooks. As Janice Gerson, an executive editor of social studies put it, "teachers do this [textbook evaluation] and nobody ever shows them how to do it. Nobody talks to them about the types of things they should be looking for." Teachers, others noted, miss the most exciting features of their texts while paying much more attention to the ancillaries of a publisher's package—instructional guides, workbooks, sample tests, and transparencies—that accompany the books free of charge. Curriculum supervisor and publishing representative David Caine described his meeting with a group of reviewers this way:

> I was assisting with a sales presentation on Tuesday. . . . My part of the presentation was to concentrate on content, what is going on in the books, what's going on in here. And there was some interest in what I was saying, but that interest was minimal compared to when we began to talk about what materials were available free with the program. Then they started writing and quizzing us very carefully. "Now, do we get six books, or do we get four books with that?" That's where the real animation came.

As noted earlier, there are many reasons textbook evaluation committees showed less interest in specific content issues. For one, time constraints reduced the likelihood of close and detailed inspection. Though critics of textbook evaluation practices refer pejoratively to the "flip test," Caine explained how flipping quickly through a text enabled evaluators to narrow a dizzying array of choices.

> What our experience has been, and I think that most people in the industry would agree, that the competition is so fierce, and teachers' interest in and time to review books is so limited, that the first step of any reviewing committee is to just cut books off the list. And they've got to get down to a list of two or three before they can really get down and really consider anything about the books. So they'll look at just about anything that can cut a book off the list. And if there is something that's a little different, a little off, something that just doesn't quite match with the others or match with a preconceived view, the books are gone. And there are lots of examples of publishers whose books have fallen to last place.

In anticipation of such tactics publishers hope to provide features with immediate appeal, which means that cosmetic details, much more than meanings and perspectives, assume importance. Again, Caine's assessment of publishers' perspective is illuminating:

If every text looked like say a novel, that there's very little inside except the type face and perhaps running heads and feets, nobody would be able to make a decision in two minutes. They'd actually have to read it. When you've got four color head, and dropped shadows, and silhouetted photographs, and things all over the place, you get an immediate impression about whether this is a friendly, usable, huggable text . . . if you haven't done absolutely the most perfect job of anticipating needs. I mean years ago nobody would have used teal as a color. But now teal is in. So everybody uses teal. If you judged wrong on what the color plate, on what everybody's going to like, you've made a terrible mistake.

When evaluating educational trends, publishers distinguish between the needs of seasoned professionals and administrators who regularly attend workshops or meetings of the National Council of Social Studies and the concerns of the average classroom teacher. While experienced educators may look for textbooks with greater depth and analysis, creative classroom exercises and stimulating prose, others feel dissatisfied with books that provide minimal instructional aid or are too difficult to get through. Contrary to theories of critical pedagogy[37] that encourage student participation and empowerment in the classroom, teachers, social studies editor Cheryl Jacobs observed, generally want books that enhance their own control over the classroom.

Part of it, especially at the lower levels [is that] teachers aren't experts on content. But they're experts on teaching so that's something they know about. They have some hands on experience with what a kid can do with a map, what is the kiss of death for presenting something, what really works, what makes them lose control of a class, what leads them astray. They're very interested in managing their class, and getting through content in a course of a day, the course of a semester, and the course of a year.

Furthermore, Jacobs also reported that many teachers are quite reluctant to encourage in-depth, critical class discussions about substantive matters.

We find in lower schools in particular, teachers are very nervous about content. When they have to teach geography you would think geography was physics. They get very nervous about it; they want you to hold their hands. They want everything there. And so they don't want you to stimulate too much discussion. They're afraid of looking silly. Particularly in any content area you get into, and you know if you look in graduate education schools and what they teach there, people who graduate with a degree in education don't have much academic background.

The notion that teachers are "very nervous about content" is consistent with how textbook committee members, described in chapter 2,

differentiated between the "philosophical concerns" they try to avoid
and what is important "education-wise," as one member put it. Teachers value features that facilitate instruction. Yet, their focus on "non-
book" issues, as director of social studies Shirley Flint described them,
greatly discourages publishers from experimenting with more creative
ideas:

> They are very much taken with features that will make their jobs easier. Now
> I think anybody would be so it's not a criticism. But it means that we tend to
> focus a lot of our attention on how we organize the teaching material,
> whether our suggestion for activities are ones that do not require an enormous
> amount of preparation time. Many of the very best kinds of activity sugges-
> tions in social studies, especially in the elementary schools, are really activity
> suggestions and non-book kinds of things. And you could give very thorough
> instructions on how to do these things. . . . But we don't do very much of
> that because we know that if we do very much of that, it'll make the book
> look like this is going to be hard to teach.

The instrumental logic that governs textbook evaluation explains
why school materials are not as challenging, stimulating, or provocative
as progressive and radical theorists suggest they should be. Linking the
influence of positivism on textbook knowledge to the "death of history," Giroux argues that school materials do not invite students to
think critically about the relationship between knowledge and power.[38]
Yet, publishers have few incentives to create books that offer diverse
perspectives and develop these kinds of skills. In fact, there are disincen-
tives to doing so, created not only or mainly by traditionalist pressure
groups, but also by teachers. Describing teachers' resistance to inquiry
approaches to learning, Gerson explained, "it's a hard way to teach."

> The information is not in the book. So it takes a huge amount of work on the
> part of teachers and a huge amount of work on the part of students to get the
> background. There's nothing wrong with critical thinking or doing a lot of
> questions, but you're talking to kids with no background. . . . There's little
> academically they can draw on . . . unless you've got a teacher who can draw
> on different sources. That could make a great class, but not every teacher can
> do it, and not every student can handle it.
>
> Those books [that recommend critical thinking] went out in a year because
> most, I say *most*, some teachers loved it, but most didn't know what to do with
> it. They have different courses in a day, different levels of kids, paperwork to
> do. It's a lot easier to use a textbook, and I don't mean that negatively.

In sum, many teachers, especially those new to the profession, have little
interest in generating controversy or dealing with uncertainty.[39]

Unstructured lesson plans, textbook exercises that encourage classroom dialogue, and discussions that elicit different answers and interpretations require time, preparation, and skills these teachers may not have.

## RISK AND INNOVATION: THE LIMITS TO RADICAL CHANGE

Publishers' perceptions that their most important customers favor familiar products affect the types of books produced in two major ways. First, publishers are unlikely to take financial risks on highly innovative texts. Flint, who earlier described the obstacles to generating new products, delineated the priorities of publishing houses this way:

> In order to make a book you have to say that there's a sixth grade course and it covers these things, and there are X number of hundred thousand kids enrolled in it, and we think we can sell it at a certain amount. It's going to cost this many dollars to make it; we can get this many dollars back, we can deliver this sort of profit. It's an economic analysis like that on all of our publishing projects. And the things that I think would be fun to do because we haven't done them yet are all in the area of "the market's not large enough."

Gerson agreed that the lack of significant innovation in the industry had to do more with a fear of potential losses than an absence of good ideas:

> You've got to find somebody who's going to buy it. All publishers have to go to a board of directors and show a profit, or there's no company. . . . There are really very few [companies] left. It's very scary as an employee because there are fewer options; it's scary for teachers because the options are fewer. We'll talk sometimes and say "that's a great idea but nobody's going to buy it."
>
> I go to meetings and textbooks are criticized. Everything is blamed on the publishers and we do books in hope of selling them. Nobody's trying to do a bad book. Nobody's trying to do a book the kids are going to hate. Everybody's trying to do a book that will please the teachers, and that'll sell. If books don't sell, it doesn't count. It just doesn't do any good.

Second, given multiple sources of feedback—selection committee preferences, sessions at professional meetings, sales representatives' reports, marketing research and focus group responses—publishers attempt to strike a balance between ideas and capabilities at the cutting edge of research and design, and traditional approaches to presenting information and graphics. They strive to identify what will be most acceptable.[40] Acceptability means keeping up with one's competitors rather than distinguishing one's product from the norm. As a result, products across companies are more similar than different. Explaining his company's strategy, Caine noted:

> So we try to walk a middle line so that teachers can use it as a baseline and spread out from it. If the teacher wants to use the text as a resource or as a basic text, and then move off into primary sources or other kinds of tests and so on, we certainly hope they do. Too few teachers do. But to be able to enable the majority of teachers to do that, the content has got to walk sort of a middle line.

Identifying a middle line is achieved partly by keeping in touch with state guidelines for textbook content. I now turn to these guidelines to assess their impact on publishing practices.

## STATE REQUIREMENTS: THE TEXAS PROCLAMATIONS

When Texas sought to establish curricular standards such as the "essential elements" in the 1980s, one writer contrasted the state-mandated reforms with the state's tradition of protecting local autonomy. He wrote:

> Now, suddenly and dramatically, the rules of the game have changed. In Texas Education Code 21.101, the state board of education has clearly defined "well-balanced curriculum," and the state has told local school boards, "Thou shalt teach it!" The code goes on to make clear that "the State Board of Education is the primary policy-making body for public education and directs the public school system."[41]

Some observers of centralized textbook adoption systems have also assumed that statewide processes exercise inordinate editorial clout over the production of schoolbook knowledge. Faced with diverse demands from many purchasers, publishers are believed to be economically motivated to satisfy the interests of Florida, California, and Texas, states that purchase a large quantity of books.[42] Suggesting that decisions in Texas influence the knowledge provided to students throughout the country, Frances FitzGerald concluded:

> In sum, the system of adoptions has a significant impact on the way Americans are taught their own history. Because of the Texas State Textbook Committee, New England children, whose ancestors heartily disapproved of the Mexican War, have grown up with heroic tales of Davy Crockett and Sam Houston.[43]

Raymond English similarly summarized Texas's impact on publishers, "when Texas prescribes, publishers jump."[44]

If state prescriptions for textbook content had a measurable ideological effect on educational materials, we would likely see their impact on the practices of textbook publishers; yet there are several reasons this influence is weaker than we might expect. Contrary to common assumptions about the state's stringent demands, an examination of Texas's textbook requirements, called proclamations, indicates that those pertaining to social studies have not provided a clear mandate or espoused a single ideology. On the contrary, Texas requirements have supported both traditional and progressive perspectives.[45]

For example, the proclamations of the late 1970s and early 1980s emphasized "patriotism and respect for recognized authority."[46] Textbooks were expected to "present positive aspects of the United States and its heritage," and exclude "selections or works which encourage or condone civil disorder, social strife, or disregard for the law."[47] Though the state required textbooks to be objective and impartial, it clearly promoted mainstream values. "Lifestyles deviating from generally accepted standards of society" were discouraged.[48]

But while the above requirements emphasized "accepted standards of society," others encouraged progressive principles of tolerance, cultural diversity, and "mutual understanding and respect."[49] One part of the proclamation stated,

> Textbooks, whenever possible, shall present varying life styles, shall treat divergent groups fairly, without stereotyping, and shall reflect the positive contributions of all individuals and groups to the American way of life. Illustrations and written material will avoid bias toward any particular life style, group, or individual and should present a wide range of goal choices and life styles.[50]

Content guidelines for history and government recognized the contributions of "various religious, national, racial, and ethnic groups' backgrounds" as well as "reliable accounts of minorities and women and their roles in American history."[51] They also promoted progressive pedagogical approaches including "historical investigation and critical thinking" as well as "end-of-chapter questions and activities to develop high level thinking skills."[52]

By granting space to competing views, the state serves its own needs as a mediating institution. As Martin Carnoy has argued, the American educational system engages in a dual process of reproduction and democratization as it addresses simultaneous demands from the business class, from social movements pushing for equality, and from movements that "feel threatened by state secularism, the advance of minorities, or the more equal role of women in society."[53] While the state responds to pressures for inclusion and legitimation, it also manages conflict by incorporating new images and ideas in ways that emphasize individual identities over class, race and gender distinctions[54] and reinforce the values of achievement and individualism associated with a dominant business culture.[55]

## IMPACT OF STATE POLICIES ON THE PRESENTATION OF KNOWLEDGE

As a result of state policies and mediation, textbook knowledge tends to be simplistic and moderate in tone. Though always ideological, it is also very bland because publishers generally manage curricular change in trivial ways. Because proclamations contain mixed messages rather than unambiguous positions, it is no wonder that publishers can use various marketing devices to fulfill the requirements of particular states. Despite being positioned as gatekeepers of knowledge, publishers, much like teachers, see themselves as removed from political struggles over school knowledge. They respond to state requirements in ways that incur the fewest potential costs, economically and ideologically. To meet the expectations of a state such as Texas, for example, publishers have included content that correlates with the Texas essential elements, but they have done so by using tactics such as labeling. Dean Lindstrom, a director of social studies for a publishing company, described this strategy as follows:

> Nowadays critical thinking, creative thinking, and higher-order thinking, these are important words at some level of the evaluation process. The way publishers respond to that is to label. . . . in fact, they'll label old programs to say they have critical thinking, but then when you come to use it, you'll see that there's really no process of critical thinking, that they have just added that label.

For illustrations, publishers might use the state's flag, a piece of recent legislation, or a photograph of a popular government official to make a special edition. In its 1986 adoption of health textbooks, the Texas State Board of Education mandated that the books include a page of state laws regarding the use of drugs and alcohol; publishers complied.

Nonetheless, according to publishers, these special editions are fairly simple to prepare. They may involve little more than highlighting pages of material with color during the printing process. Downplaying the significance of creating multiple editions of a text, Flint said,

You're running your book, and you stop the press, change the blue plate, and keep going and you've got your Texas teacher' edition. So it's a way of customizing the book for Texas teachers that does not incur an enormous amount of expense to the publisher. It's a marketing device really.

Others concurred that they could easily address some state requirements by including different pictures, people, or maps where appropriate.[56] But they distinguished between these kinds of additions and content-related alterations pertaining to perspectives and ideologies. Curriculum director Caine said:

> We still do two different editions, but not because of a difference in viewpoint. It's more to get more information about a state into [a] particular book. We can teach math skills with say a road map using any city in the United States as the example. So for the Texas edition, we certainly put Dallas in there instead of Portland. For an Oregon edition, we'd certainly put Portland in there. It's more that sort of thing. I don't know of any book that's published for a state because it has a certain point of view.

Content prescriptions also affect a book's organization—its sequence, scope, and selection of material—for each grade level, but not, as Tim Peterson, executive director of social studies, also noted, the book's message.[57]

> In the past it [Texas] has had great influence on curriculum. But not necessarily in terms of viewpoint. For example, in the U.S. history market in Texas you're going to create two books—one that goes through the Civil War, or through reconstruction, and one high school book for tenth and eleventh grade from 1865 to the present. That influences how you put the books together, and subsequently, what you offer to the national market. However, that doesn't have an effect on the viewpoint of the book.

Certainly, parents, interest groups, and others who critique textbooks would disagree with publishers' claims. Issues of inclusion and exclusion can affect the perspective of a book. That is precisely why activists contest textbook knowledge. Publishers, however, see a clear difference between the arrangement and presentation of textbook material and the meanings the book conveys.

## CONCLUSION: TEXTBOOKS AND THE LOWEST COMMON DENOMINATOR

Textbook publishers are often criticized for compromising substance and quality to achieve broad appeal and for sacrificing individual writing styles and interpretations to readability formulas. Like writers for television who use "stick dialogue more than story, schematic story line more than complexity, and, in comedy, jokes more than consistency or intensity of character or situation," publishers, focusing on "the facts," of who, what, and where, produce educational materials that read more like encyclopedias than works of scholarship.[58] Because many topics and events must be covered to meet different state requirements, books rarely provide sufficient detail or an in-depth analysis of perspectives, nor do they express an individual author's viewpoint. "I don't think a publisher in the last twenty years has published an unsolicited manuscript," Henry Graham, a national consultant for a publishing company, explained.

> I mean, publishers decide what they can publish, and then go look for authors to do it. You know of an up-and-coming department chairman in a psychology school, or your sales representative says "watch this person, this lady, she's given talks and so forth," and you ask her to join your team. And you listen to all of those things, but you do your own research. And you say, "be sure you do this, be sure you do that." I'm not saying the author is completely anonymous. But their role is again, not like their role in the trade book or anything.

Books for the secondary school market generally reflect the input of numerous individuals hired for specific purposes such as their expertise on minorities or labor.

But while academic consultants confirm that so-called social issues such as diversity are included, editors assume responsibility for tailoring the final products. Note, in the following quote, that Caine is concerned more about using a consistent label to describe Native Americans than about how Native Americans are actually presented in textbooks.

> Our authors don't get the guidelines so much, because we want them to generate, certainly we have over the past few years, encouraged them to generate much more lively, sparkling prose, and we feel that we won't get that if we give them too many restrictions right out front. So the authors generally don't get those guidelines, the editors do. And the editors will make decisions about how to . . . generally those guidelines are social issues, and issues of consistency. Do you call them American Indians, or do you call them Native Americans. And we have to make a decision so there's some consistency. Those guidelines are passed out to the editors, and we don't bother our authors with trying to be consistent about things like that.

Because a publisher's success is measured largely in terms of market shares rather than substantive merit, textbooks have been described as a form of commodified culture,[59] the implications of which are described in Todd Gitlin's description of the television industry:

> Network executives often say that their problem is simple. Their tradition, in a sense, is the search for steady profits. They want, above all, to put on the air shows best calculated to accumulate maximum reliable audiences. Maximum audiences attract maximum dollars for advertisers, and advertiser dollars, are, after all, the network's objective . . . Quality and explicit ideology count for very little.[60]

Similarly, decisions about textbook content—what knowledge is presented and how—are not necessarily based on educational philosophy or a coherent notion of what constitutes good education. Rather, avoiding controversy and providing books familiar to teachers matter most as Lindstrom said:

> In government, Magruder's *Government* did not make the list the last time. But I guess it made the list in 85–86. . . . That's revised every year. And it's become *the* American government book. I'm not sure what percent of the market it has, but it was once the dominant book. [One year] it didn't make the list in Texas, and when it came up for the second evaluation six years later, people just wanted to get it again. They were so familiar with it, and had come to rely on it.

In spite of the analogies that can be drawn between mass culture products and school textbooks,[61] some publishers contend that their industry accurately speaks to, but does not manipulate, consumer preferences; rather, they are in tune with teachers' needs because many people employed in school textbook divisions have worked in school classrooms.[62] Flint argued that however narrow the preferences of teachers may be, they are certainly more sophisticated, and at least more tasteful, than those of television audiences:

> The audience for textbooks is not the audience that the television program's aimed at. And that's a real big difference. I mean, your audience is the educators of this country. Now maybe we could have, we could argue about what the hell does that say about the audience of educators in our country. But I think you'd have to say first, that I don't think you'd find that the quality of textbooks has sunk to the level of the quality of [television]. By a long shot you would not find that the case. There may be some things that are bland, there may be some things that are not as intellectually as exciting as they could be, but I don't believe you've got sentimentality. I don't think you've got grossness . . . there's no pandering at all. In fact, quite the opposite, because the audience are school teachers, there might not be quite enough of it, of the blood and guts of history. You know we never tell the kids in history books

about the sex lives of the major figures. They don't learn that until they get to
college.

Caine asserted that publishers behave proactively and can sometimes
be credited with leading the educational profession in a progressive
direction, especially on social issues. But while his view presents a different take on the role of publishers as leaders, he readily acknowledged
that new approaches must accommodate a very diverse set of interests;
as a result, alternative ideas often do not look at all innovative once they
are tailored to the market. When push comes to shove, he focuses his
attention primarily on finding solutions to existing and potential classroom problems because he is situated in an organization motivated by
commercial interests. Here, Caine reverts to the position of marketing
expert.

> So to some degree it's what the customers want, but it's more anticipating
> what the customer may want or even getting a pretty good idea of what the
> customer's dissatisfaction is, and then coming up with a solution for it. That's
> when we're most successful, when we can identify that our teachers or stu-
> dents or somebody is very much dissatisfied with something. They don't even
> know what the solution is, and then we come up with it. *That's* when we're
> most successful.
>
> In that regard, it's not special interest group pressures, it's not even paying
> attention to what's going on at conferences or what's being written in the
> journals, or what the content issues are, but what is it that would make a
> teacher feel more successful.

If innovation takes place, it is most likely designed to affect classroom
practice rather than the ideological messages textbooks contain. The
purpose of concepts such as diversity is likely to get lost in the multiple
strategies publishers use to sell their products. Lindstrom's comment on
how his company deals with inclusiveness is telling.

> In the course of our developing a program, when we're selecting photos or
> when we're writing specifications for photos to be taken, we, at that point,
> say we want, you know, an African-American family, we want a Latino family,
> we want this that or the other thing. So that when we're putting it together,
> we're tracking the racial and ethnic mix.

As a result of these practices, high school textbook knowledge tends
to present different groups and their experiences in tokenistic ways. The
transmission of knowledge in this format is insensitive to nuance and
complexity. Even by the mid-1980s when discourse on multicultural
education began to expand, curricular materials conveyed the meaning

of constructs such as African Americans or Asian Americans in the simplest of terms. Ignoring variations within these groups, they tended to treat categories of race and ethnicity as uncomplicated classifications. Thus, a textbook picture of golfer Nancy Lopez was supposed to stand for Hispanic America.

Although the competing views voiced at textbook hearings represent struggles to define whose knowledge counts and whose cultures should be affirmed, these issues are peripheral considerations in the web of professional, organizational, and commercial factors that shape the production of textbook knowledge, moderate the impact of the culture wars, and dilute the meaning and significance of ideas such as multicultural education and diversity. Teachers' perceived instructional needs dictate publishing strategies. Despite the sociological assumption that knowledge, power, and social interests are inextricably linked, decision makers and institutional practices operate in ways that mask this link.

## NOTES

Portions of this chapter were based on one of my earlier articles—"Evaluating the Content of Textbooks: Public Interests and Professional Authority," *Sociology of Education* 64 (January 1991): 11–18.

1. Based on comments made in textbook committee deliberations, the following is a sample of positive and negative criteria that shaped committee members' textbook evaluations:

good for the low level student, reading charts and maps are easy to understand, vocabulary printed at beginning of each chapter, short chapters, well-written, introductory outline, italicized vocabulary, timelines, illustrations good, has received good feedback in classroom use, well-coordinated, challenging writing, promotes good self-concept for slow readers, bad glossary, meets multitude of needs, good planning strategies, three levels of testing, includes resource materials, readings are given at end of each chapter, is short but informative, adaptable to low level student without talking down.

Books have similar questions to those on basic skills tests, it is the opinion of the Texas Council for Social Studies that this book be recommended, Watergate coverage good, doesn't invalidate negative aspects of history, shows dilemmas as presented to the country, [includes] landmark cases (*Dred Scott, Brown v. Board of Education*), exciting, appeals to the gifted, covers the Constitution and Declaration of Independence.

[includes] critical thinking skills, list of museums and art galleries, stress on patriotism, students are motivated to see what's next, balanced treatment of ethnic groups, gives profiles of presidency; difficult to teach from, chapters contain too many interruptions, unappealing use of colors on maps.

2. See Harriet Bernstein, "The New Politics of Textbook Adoption," *Phi Delta Kappan* (March 1985): 463–66; Bruce DeSilva, "Schoolbooks: A Question of Quality," reprint of a series published in the *Hartford Courant*, 15–18 June 1986, 1–20; J. Dan Marshall, "With a Little Help from Some Friends: Publishers, Protesters, and Texas Textbook Decisions," in *The Politics of the Textbook*, ed. Michael W. Apple and Linda K. Christian-Smith, 56–77 (New York: Routledge, 1991).

3. Sherry Keith, "Choosing Textbooks: A Study of Instructional Materials Selection Processes for Public Education," *Book Research Quarterly* 1, no. 2 (Summer 1985): 24–37.

4. State Textbook Committee Chair Vidal Trevino represented the committee at the state board hearings in November 1986.

5. Stanley Aronowitz and Henry A. Giroux, *Education Still Under Siege*, 2d ed. (Westport, Conn.: Bergin & Garvey, 1993), 41.

6. Aronowitz and Giroux, *Education*, 40.

7. Michael W. Apple, *Education and Power* (Boston: Routledge & Kegan Paul, 1982).

8. Aronowitz and Giroux, *Education*, 37–38.

9. Aronowitz and Giroux, *Education*, 34. The authors note how "theories of teaching are increasingly technicized and standardized in the interest of efficiency and the management and control of discrete forms of knowledge."

10. Henry A. Giroux, *Ideology, Culture and the Process of Schooling* (Philadelphia: Temple University Press, 1981), 43.

11. Apple, *Education and Power*, 157.

12. Giroux, *Ideology, Culture and the Process of Schooling*, 53.

13. Michael Apple, *Ideology and Curriculum* (London: Routledge & Kegan Paul, 1979), 107. Also see p. 146. Apple describes the detrimental impact of prepackaged materials on skills once valued in teaching. Also see Aronowitz and Giroux, *Education*, 41. They describe educators as being " 'situated' within curricula approaches and instructional management schemes that reduce their roles to either implementing or receiving the goals and objectives of publishers, outside experts, and others far removed from the specificities of daily classroom life."

14. See Giroux, *Ideology*, 153. Giroux has argued that technical rationality and a "culture of positivism" strongly influence how schoolteachers understand their role as mediators of knowledge. "Students in teacher education," he writes, "find themselves operating out of predefined categories and styles of thought that make curriculum appear to have a life of its own" (153). These programs, he argues, do not provide the conceptual tools teachers need "in order to view knowledge as problematic, as a historically conditioned, socially constructed phenomenon" (155).

15. John W. Meyer and W. Richard Scott, *Organizational Environments: Ritual and Rationality* (Beverly Hills: Sage, 1983).

16. Michael D. Cohen and James G. March, *Leadership and Ambiguity* (New York: McGraw-Hill, 1974).

17. Daniel Chambliss, "Nursing Ethics" (Ph.D. diss., Yale University, 1982).

18. The Texas State Board of Education meets in November to approve the textbook committee's recommended list of books. Several representatives of the committee, and sometimes the entire committee, attend and respond to questions from the board.

19. Meyer and Scott, *Organizational Environments*, 234.

20. Meyer and Scott, *Organizational Environments*, 234.

21. John Meyer, "Organizations as Ideological Systems" in *Leadership and Organizational Culture*, ed. Thomas Sergiovanni and John E. Corbally (Urbana: University of Illinois Press, 1984), 189.

22. John W. Meyer and Brian Rowan, "The Structure of Educational Organizations," in Marshall W. Meyer and Associates, *Environments and Organizations* (San Francisco: Jossey-Bass, 1978), 79.

23. Gaye Tuchman, *Edging Women Out* (New Haven, Conn.: Yale University Press, 1989); Walter W. Powell, *Getting into Print* (Chicago: University of Chicago Press, 1985); Louis A. Coser, Charles Kadushin, and Walter W. Powell, *Books: The Culture and Commerce of Publishing* (New York: Basic, 1982); Gaye Tuchman, *Making News* (New York: Free Press, 1978); Todd Gitlin, *Inside Prime Time* (New York: Pantheon, 1983); and Chandra Mukerji and Michael Schudson, eds., *Rethinking Popular Culture* (Berkeley: University of California Press, 1991).

24. Powell, *Getting into Print*, 128–160.

25. Coser et al., *Books: The Culture and Commerce*, 269–282.

26. Janet Wolff, *The Social Production of Art* (New York: St. Martin's, 1981).

27. Pierre Bourdieu, *The Field of Cultural Production* (New York: Columbia University Press, 1993).

28. Tuchman, *Edging Women Out*, 23.

29. Bourdieu, *Field of Cultural Production*, 115.

30. Lewis Coser et al., *Books: The Culture and Commerce*, 7.

31. Michael W. Apple, "The Culture and Commerce of the Textbook," *Journal of Curriculum Studies* 17 (1985): 154.

32. Apple, "Culture and Commerce," 155.

33. Myra Sadker and David Sadker, *Failing at Fairness* (New York: Touchstone, 1994), 72.

34. See Mukerji and Schudson, eds., *Rethinking Popular Culture*, 32–33. The authors write: "organizations respond not to their 'real' environments but to their perception of the environment. Even in the most pragmatic organizations, culture—in the form of traditions, ideologies, and presuppositions—enters into the formulation of problems. The 'bottom line' is no less a 'cultural' product than other humanly constructed lines (national borders, time zone demarcations, or newspaper deadlines)."

35. Wolff, *Social Production of Art*, 47.

36. Robert Follett, "The School Textbook Adoption Process," *Book Research Quarterly* 1, no. 2 (Summer 1985): 22.

37. Henry A. Giroux, "Schooling as a Form of Cultural Politics: Toward a Pedagogy of and for Difference," in *Critical Pedagogy, the State, and Cultural Struggle*, ed. Henry Giroux and Peter McLaren (New York: SUNY Press, 1989), 125–51.

38. Giroux, *Ideology*, 37–62. Giroux is referring to the presentation of knowledge as objective, unquestionable facts.

39. James Loewen, *Lies My Teacher Told Me* (New York: New Press, 1995), 280.

40. Powell, *Getting into Print*, 29. Powell writes, "There is little variation in the production process even though the subject matter of the books may differ greatly.

With such high stakes involved, most houses opt for a fairly conservative strategy, and there is a good deal of imitation of competitor's products."

41. Michael Killian, "Local Control—Vanishing Myth in Texas." *Phi Delta Kappan* (November 1984): 193.

42. Roger Farr and Michael A. Tulley, "Do Adoption Committees Perpetuate Mediocre Textbooks?" *Phi Delta Kappan* (March 1985): 467–71.

43. Frances FitzGerald, *America Revised* (New York: Vintage, 1980), 34.

44. Raymond English, "The Politics of Textbook Adoption," *Phi Delta Kappan* (December 1980), 277. See also Wayne A. Moyer, "How Texas Rewrote Your Textbooks," *The Science Teacher* (January 1985), 23.

45. The belief that Texas requirements are predominantly conservative is more widespread. See Mary Ansaldo, former vice president of Ginn & Co., paraphrased in DeSilva, "Schoolbooks," 15. Ansaldo said, "And to sell social studies and reading books in Texas . . . it is important to strike a patriotic chord, to show that bad conduct by children is always punished, to frown on peaceful protests against the government, and 'to say that Russia is a bad place to live.' "

46. The examples noted are from the general textbook content provisions of the *Proclamation of the State Board of Education Advertising for Bids on Textbooks No. 56*, Texas Education Agency, Austin, Texas, 1980. For a reprint of the general provisions, see J. Dan Marshall, "State-Level Textbook Selection Reform: Toward the Recognition of Fundamental Control" in *Textbooks in American Society*, ed. Philip G. Altbach, Gail P. Kelly, Hugh G. Petrie, and Lois Weis, (Albany, N.Y.: SUNY Press, 1991), 135.

47. Marshall, "State-Level Textbook Selection Reform," 135.

48. Marshall, "State-Level Textbook Selection Reform," 136.

49. Marshall, "State-Level Textbook Selection Reform," 136.

50. Marshall, "State-Level Textbook Selection Reform," 136.

51. *Proclamation No. 54*, Texas Education Agency, Austin, Texas, 1978, 45.

52. *Proclamation No. 54*, Texas Education Agency, Austin, Texas, 1978, 46.

53. Martin Carnoy, "Education, State, and Culture in American Society," in *Critical Pedagogy, the State, and Cultural Struggle,* ed. Henry Giroux and Peter McLaren (Albany, N.Y.: SUNY Press, 1989), 7.

54. Carnoy, "Education, State, and Culture," 12.

55. Carnoy, "Education, State, and Culture," 4.

56. Textbook critics would point out that multiple requirements from different states, even if trivial with respect to ideological perspective, do have negative consequences for the form that textbooks take. The formulation of mandates as lists of required facts affects textbook production and selection in numerous ways. Although many evaluation committees expect textbooks to include particular facts or events, they do not necessarily pay attention to how the material is presented or to other qualities associated with the intellectual merit of a book. See Farr and Tulley, "Do Adoption Committees Perpetuate Mediocre Textbooks?" 467–71; and Keith, "Choosing Textbooks," 24–37. The presentation of content has become a more important issue since the turbulent 1970s; however, textbook critics regard publishers' attempts to revise conventional narratives as being trivial and mechanical. Attempting to satisfy multiple requirements from different states and localities, publishers tend to produce voluminous books fashioned much like encyclopedias.

57. In the late 1980s, California, another large adoption state, made its content prescriptions more specific, and increased its efforts to ensure compliance. Some publishers felt these mandates had greater potential to affect the perspective or viewpoint of textbooks. See California State Board of Education, "History-Social Science Framework for California Public Schools Kindergarten through Grade Twelve," (Sacramento, Calif.: California State Department of Education, 1988).

58. Gitlin, *Inside Prime Time*, 83.

59. Apple, "Culture and Commerce of the Textbook," 147–62.

60. Todd Gitlin, *Inside Prime Time*, 25.

61. While the entertainment industry strives to please the widest range of tastes and preferences, textbook publishers seek to appease the broadest range of instructional needs and student abilities. And like program creators who are often criticized for low cultural standards, publishers have been charged with producing watered-down textbooks. Just as popular stars or authors are hired to attract audiences and readers, textbook publishers include the names of noted scholars on their covers. Television producers, movie moguls, and trade book publishers search for a potential blockbuster series, a summer or Christmas box office hit, or best-selling novel; textbook publishers seek their largest profits from the sale of series for subjects such as reading, which have consistent demand and are used in sequence by grade-specific populations of students. These contracts are especially lucrative in large markets.

62. DeSilva, "Schoolbooks," 4.

# 4

# Cultural Politics and Curricular Battles in New York

By the late 1980s, agendas for diversity in education began to move curriculum reforms beyond the language of inclusion that had dominated textbook debates in Texas to a discourse of multiculturalism grounded in concepts of identity formation and validation. In this chapter, I turn to two sites of curricular struggle in New York State and New York City to show how the terms of debates shifted over time and to examine the impact of cultural politics on a second form of official knowledge.

Curricular struggles in New York, like textbook battles in Texas, were rooted in competing values, meanings, and ideas. Yet, the issues at stake in New York also differed from those in Texas in critical ways. When progressive petitioners in Texas pressured the state to validate the experiences and accomplishments of women and racial and ethnic minorities, their expectations reflected a logic of inclusion and representation. In other words, they wanted individuals and groups neglected in traditional narratives of history to be recognized as part of the American story. According to these terms, school materials should acknowledge women and minorities for their successes and contributions as defined by mainstream norms of acculturation and achievement. The goal of inclusion, which dominated multicultural discourse through the mid-1980s, was consistent with a melting-pot theory that minimized group distinctions and focused on individual merits and attainments. By representing ethnic groups such as Chinese Americans with references to architect I. M. Pei, textbooks recognized minorities for fitting in, and for affirming the ideology of equal opportunity in American society.

## A NEW MODEL OF PLURALISM

By contrast, curricular reforms in New York State prescribed a new model of pluralism intended not merely to integrate previously

excluded groups into dominant versions of history, but to recognize distinctly different cultural identities as being meaningful and equally valid.
In 1990, New York State's Commissioner of Education Thomas Sobol
appointed a social studies review and development committee to recommend changes in the state's curriculum that would increase students'
understanding of diverse cultures, identities, and histories in American
society and throughout the world.[1] Consistent with the tenets of critical
multicultural theories, the committee's ninety-seven-page report, *One
Nation, Many Peoples: A Declaration of Cultural Interdependence,*[2] acknowledged "a fundamental change in the image of what a resident of the
United States is" and rejected "previous ideals of assimilation to an
Anglo-American model." Curriculum planners also encouraged "a
more tolerant, inclusive, and realistic vision of American identity," one
"marked by respect for pluralism and awareness of the virtues of diversity."[3]

The new model of pluralism would, in short, celebrate the diversity
of different groups and cultures so that all students would see themselves
as an important part of social studies lessons. According to *One Nation,
Many Peoples,* schools would encourage students to ask questions such
as the following: Who am I? What is/are my cultural heritage(s)? Why
should I be proud of it/them? Why should I develop an understanding
of and respect for my own culture(s), language(s), religion, and national
origin(s)? Why should I develop an understanding of and respect for the
cultures, the languages, the religions, and the national origins of others?
What is an American? What holds us together as a nation?[4]

By legitimizing, affirming, and promoting differences, these curricular reforms, at least on the surface, reversed the established view that
schools must assimilate young people, especially immigrant children,
who presumably need unambiguous prescriptions of what is good and
bad, proper and improper, and worthy of being known. This view, as
historian David Nasaw has shown, has been central to public education
since the formation of common schools in the late 1800s.

> A common school education would be a moral education. By making the
> population more moral, the common schools would also make it more docile,
> more tractable, less given to social discord, disruption and disobedience. The
> young would be taught to vote right and to pray right, to distinguish the
> responsible citizen from the demagogue, the false from the true, in matters of
> state and of church.[5]

Education, at least for the masses, meant learning a body of facts and a
set of values that reflected a unified concept of national identity. Cul-

tural diversity was a problem to be remedied by consensus, centralization, and assimilation.

Furthermore, New York's curricular proposals appeared to mark an important shift in thinking not only about diversity in American culture but also the students' role in producing knowledge. Consistent with theories of critical pedagogy, reform ideas drew on student experiences as a source of educational motivation and empowerment and conceived of young people as individuals with specific interests defined by their gender, race, and sexual identity.[6] The reforms offer an empirical referent with which to assess the promise of realizing these ideals in curricular policy.

My argument, though, is that while state officials seemed poised to take a proactive step in moving discourse about diversity to a different plane, the transformative possibilities of new ideas were curtailed in processes of policy making and negotiation. At both the state and local levels, resistance to alternative ideas and practices of mediation impeded the realization of curricular transformations and produced outcomes quite similar to those in Texas even though the focus of struggle and the organization and dynamics of decision making differed across cases. The discourse surrounding curricular struggles in New York signified the increasing legitimacy of multicultural education, but the way in which multicultural education came to be defined, understood, and practiced fell short of radical ideas of educational change.

## CONTESTING THE SIGNIFICANCE
## OF ETHNICITY

The objectives of *One Nation, Many Peoples* and the substantive and pedagogical assumptions on which they were based drew criticism from those who questioned the value of increasing attention to diversity in school curricula. Rejecting the premise of multicultural education, one high school teacher said, "I certainly wouldn't back a report that tried to give all cultures equal weight. That's a distortion of history,"[7] while another argued that "the movement towards diversity is an attempt to trash white European history. . . . I feel bad about students' being shortchanged for somebody else's political agenda," he said.[8] Cautioning against the hasty acceptance of reform aims, then Governor Mario Cuomo said, "While all students will gain from inclusion of different ethnic perspectives, this ought not become a rationale for denying the

European influence on many of our fundamental and enduring institutions."[9]

The strongest source of resistance to *One Nation, Many Peoples* came from a minority among the state's social studies review and development committee that argued that the current enthusiasm for recognizing differences threatened the nation's cultural unity. Emphasizing the need for common traditions that would link, rather than divide, a diverse American society, Kenneth Jackson, professor of history and social sciences at Columbia University, observed:

> Leaving aside the debatable question of whether or not we in fact have conformity (from Broadway in New York to Broadway in Los Angeles we can easily find more diversity than exists anywhere else on earth) or whether earlier immigrant groups were "required" to "shed their specific cultural differences in order to be considered Americans," I would argue that it is politically and intellectually unwise for us to attack the traditions, customs, and values which attracted immigrants to these shores in the first place. The people of the United States will recognize, even if this committee does not, that every viable nation has to have a common culture to survive in peace.[10]

Refusing to support the premise of *One Nation, Many Peoples*, Jackson said that "within any single country, one culture must be accepted as the standard." Instead, he argued, the curriculum proposals "seemed to disparage 'Anglo' conformity."[11]

Similarly, historian Arthur Schlesinger Jr., who later authored a book entitled *The Disuniting of America*, objected to *One Nation, Many People's* neglect of America's roots in European culture. In a "Statement of the Committee of Scholars in Defense of History," coauthored with educator Diane Ravitch and signed by twenty-six other scholars, Schlesinger opposed a curriculum that divided racial and ethnic groups while failing to stress their unifying ideals.[12] Educational reformers, he suggested, were proposing curricular agendas purely for the sake of helping students feel better about themselves. The acquisition of academic knowledge, a primary purpose of education, had become secondary to an alternative aim, the social and psychological well-being of the individual.

Critiques of *One Nation, Many Peoples* focused not only on issues of pluralism and unity, but also on assumptions about the importance and meaning of ethnicity in American life. Schlesinger contested the curriculum's message that "ethnicity is the defining experience for most Americans, that ethnic ties are permanent and indelible, that the division into ethnic groups establishes the basic structure of American society and that a main objective of public education should be the protection, strengthening, celebration and perpetuation of ethnic origins and identities."[13] Ethnic subcultures, he argued, should be maintained in the family, the church and community, but not in public schools.[14] Likewise, Harvard educator Nathan Glazer, who later wrote the book, *We Are All Multiculturalists Now*, warned against "the hypostatization of race, ethnic group, culture, people" or in simpler terms, the tendency to "make into, or regard as, a separate and distinct substance . . . to assume a reality."[15] He wrote:

> When we speak of "multiculturalism," we should be aware there are no fully distinct cultures in the United States, aside from American culture. We should not make of something labile, changeable, flexible and variable—the cultures people bring with them to the United States or develop as variants of our common American culture—something hard and definite and unchanging, something that establishes itself as a distinct and permanent element in American society and polity. That is not the way our society works, or should work.[16]

According to these views, the presumption that individuals inherit certain cultural traits, values, and predilections made credible a form of "cultural geneticism" that restricted individual behaviors to burdensome scripts.[17] These arguments foreshadowed debates over identity politics that would continue to occupy academic discourse between the Left and the Right throughout the 1990s.

## CURRICULAR NEGOTIATIONS AND INSTITUTIONAL PROCESSES: THE DILUTION OF CRITICAL MULTICULTURAL AGENDAS

Although the Organization of American Historians supported the tenets of New York's reform proposals and argued against the traditional view of American society as having "a wholly singular and static cultural heritage,"[18] opposition to new notions of pluralism moved curricular planners toward consensus and moderation in their deliberations over *One Nation, Many Peoples*.[19] Former social studies committee member Catherine Cornbleth recalled that "political sensitivity was manifest in repeated reviews of committee language to eliminate 'red flags' and any appearance of extremism." "More conservative committee members," she observed, "seemed to have played on this concern to push their positions."[20] For example, in the course of reviewing drafts of *One Nation, Many Peoples*, "Jackson reminded committee members to be aware of the larger political context, which he characterized as a growing backlash (against multiculturalism). To reach people in the middle, Jackson urged paying attention to language and being positive wherever possible, rather than negative."[21]

Dissenting views had noticeable effects on the framing of multicultural objectives. Ultimately, Commissioner Sobol endorsed the report but adopted what he called a "moderate, common-sense position," intended to appease both sides. Syllabi for the study of United States history, Sobol concluded, should develop an "understanding and appreciation of the democratic and moral values of our common culture" *and* an "understanding and appreciation of the history and culture of the various major ethnic and cultural groups which comprise American society."[22] Their purpose is to "cultivate 'multiple perspectives' "[23] *and* "teach our common traditions,"[24] as well as to ensure "that all students, whatever their race or ethnicity, see how they and their ancestors have shared in the building of the country and have a stake in its success."[25] Nonetheless, he noted, the curriculum should "avoid 'hypostatization,' "[26] the term committee member Glazer had used when he cautioned against treating groups as if they were composed of a "distinct and separate substance."[27] Like reform critics, Sobol opposed giving too much attention to ethnic identities or using the curriculum to achieve therapeutic aims. He would *not recommend*: excluding the traditions of the West, an Afrocentric curriculum, ethnic cheerleading and separatism, distorting history, a curriculum focused on self-esteem, or a study of American history based on ethnicity or culture alone.[28] In August 1991, The New York State Board of Regents voted twelve to three to allow Sobol to continue his plans for reform and to draft changes in the state's syllabi for history and social studies.[29] But as indicated by the resolutions cited above, these plans reflected a compromise unlikely to produce a basis for radical change.

The state appointed a Curriculum and Assessment Committee to carry out the goals of *One Nation, Many People* and to specify learning outcomes in keeping with state mandates for diversity.[30] However, disagreements between those sympathetic to the perspectives of multicultural critics and those who supported a more progressive view of diversity in American culture restricted the terms of discussion. Observing how resistance to a new model of pluralism affected the substance of committee agendas, former member Cornbleth noted that by January 1994, "diversity and unity were now on a par."[31] Only a minority among the committee took interest in transformative ideas, ideas that would have moved the curriculum in a more radical direction. Cornbleth recalled:

> For most committee members, the pluralism-unity question, as it had been defined by the neo-nativists, and their supporters in the America debate, was most salient. Few seemed to understand or take an interest in the larger multicultural issues such as the different assumptions and implications of additive and revisionist compared with transformative versions of multiculturalism.
>
> Very few active committee members seemed to advocate a transformative multicultural position and reach out effectively to others in the course of committee meetings. Transformative ideas and approaches made modest headway, at least temporarily, in the smaller working and writing groups.[32]

Instead, committee members, reluctant to implement radical reforms, focused on "how to provide varied multicultural examples without becoming too prescriptive or incorporating what one committee member had called 'too much' multiculturalism. 'Too much' multiculturalism was defined implicitly as whatever would require major revision of what teachers taught or whatever would prompt renewed controversy."[33]

## PROCESSES OF STATE MEDIATION

As noted in chapter 3, when states promulgate curricular policies their efforts commonly evoke fears of state control, centralization, and bureaucracy. Whether these policies pertain to textbook material or curricular objectives, state initiatives and reform agendas suggest rigidly enforced mandates and sometimes dramatic change. When New York State formulated its report, *One Nation, Many Peoples*, for example, some observers viewed the plan as a "radically different program for public education."[34]

Consistent with multicultural aims, the authors of *One Nation, Many Peoples* clearly sought to make educational knowledge more relevant to diverse student experiences and characteristics. However, as was the case with Texas's textbook proclamations, I found that the aims of New York's curricular plan fell short of transforming notions of identity or reconstructing knowledge of group relations and social inequality. Instead, the report's objectives reflected the contradictory goals of a democratic capitalist system.[35] As Michael Apple has observed, the state forms "accords or compromises that incorporate certain progressive tendencies over knowledge and power while at the same time recontextualizing them so that they do not threaten the overall basis of power over culture and economy."[36] Through a process of accommodation, curricular change is limited to reformations rather than transformations of official knowledge.

Passages from *One Nation, Many Peoples* exemplify these accords. On the one hand, the statement below encourages educators to recognize the diverse backgrounds of their students, an aim that is central to multicultural education. Challenging the conventional assumption that mainstream experiences will resonate with every child in a classroom, it emphasizes sensitivity to multiple experiences.

> All too often when communities are perceived as monolithic, it is common to teach from one perspective, usually that of the so-called dominant culture. For example, in the primary grades children examine neighborhoods and communities. Educators need to be aware that many of the typical features cited for study (such as banks, government buildings, department stores, and other major economic institutions) may not necessarily be present in inner-city or rural communities. Students need to be exposed to the strengths and potential of what does exist in their community, despite obstacles such as drugs and high visibility of crime. What does exist in the students' immediate real world should be used to help them become more aware of and sensitive to their civic responsibilities and possibilities in building their community.[37]

On the other hand, in contrast to the aims of critical multicultural theorists, these curricular recommendations remain consistent with meritocratic values of individualism and achievement. Presumably, students will regard the positive attributes of their communities as a source of hope and pride, but the lesson provides no explanation for why the primary economic institutions of the larger society are *not visible* in their communities. Missing is a basis for understanding why communities differ as they do—in resources, infrastructure, and social problems. Instead, the primary message is that individual actions should be used to remedy systemic problems that are portrayed as local problems. Students, it is implied, are responsible for overcoming the disadvantages of their backgrounds and improving the conditions of their own communities. Thus, the passage affirms a liberal pluralist, rather than a critical, multicultural perspective. The dominant culture is identified without being implicated.

In a similar vein, while *One Nation, Many Peoples* endorses principles consistent with multicultural aims, these principles are also couched in a language of responsibility. Social studies should promote democracy (bridging the gap between reality and ideals), diversity (understanding and respecting others and oneself), economic and social justice (understanding personal and social responsibility for economic and social systems, and for their effects), globalism (recognizing interdependence and world citizenship), ecological balance (recognizing responsibility for the global neighborhood), ethics and values (the pursuit of fairness and search for responsibility), and the individual and society (seeing oneself as a participant in society.) Although these principles include diversity, as intended, they are rooted in traditional conceptions of social studies education as a foundation for good citizenship and, as mentioned several times, individual responsibility.

Finally, the authors of *One Nation, Many Peoples* sought to assure students of the value of their identities by decentering knowledge and referring to minority groups in affirmative terms. They advised replacing "Far East" with "East Asia" and "Middle East" with "Southwest Asia and North Africa." They also suggested replacing "minorities" in America with "world's majorities." Explaining their rationale, curriculum planners wrote:

> Perhaps the most persistent and fundamental language problem in the teaching of social studies is the use of the terms "minority," "minorities," "minority persons" or "minority groups." Although commonly used, such terms nonetheless establish in the minds of all students inaccurate perceptions of the world and, increasingly, of our own nation. If social studies are to be taught from a global perspective, many of the so-called "minorities" in America are more accurately described as part of the world's majorities, a profoundly important point for young Americans who will come to maturity in the next century.[38]

In spite of the committee's intent, the proposal fails to provide a reconstructed view of majority-minority relations. Though mindful of the need to avoid dated terms "such as 'third world,' 'Negro,' and 'Oriental' "[39] the passage above neglects an opportunity to enhance students' understanding of the structure of dominant and subordinate relations throughout U.S. history. Just as a logic of inclusion restricted the progressive possibilities of Texas's textbook requirements, the curricular mission of *One Nation, Many Peoples* was sensitive to how individuals might feel about their differences, but remained silent about the ways in which differences factor into group struggle.[40] In short, the new model of pluralism recognized group identities, but it did not situate group experiences in a broader context of social relations and social structure.[41] Minority students might learn to be proud of their heritage, but neither they nor their majority peers would necessarily understand the relationship between group identities, social inequality, and discrimination.

New York's reform goals moved beyond issues of inclusion; in so doing, the state raised new questions about American identity and the role of schools in promoting cultural diversity. However, regardless of some reformers' original intentions, the state's new ideals for teaching social studies ultimately failed to establish a body of official knowledge that would provide the perspective and level of critique that are central to theories of critical multiculturalism and pedagogy.

Finally, the impact of a new model of pluralism was further attenuated in the course of translating curricular policy into practice. As in Texas, where issues of instruction and classroom management dominated textbook evaluation and selection, the New York State Education Department gave highest priority to curricular objectives far removed from specific issues of content. By producing "curriculum, instruction, and assessment frameworks instead of content-focused syllabi, and Regents exams involving 'performances' as well as multiple-choice and essay questions," the state strayed from its original focus on recognizing diversity.[42] Even so, "More than two and one-half years after the New York State Board of Regents adopted 'Understanding Diversity,'" which was based on *One Nation, Many Peoples,* the new agenda "still had not been translated into operational policies for curriculum and instruction, assessment, or teacher education and certification."[43] As of 1997, the course guidelines for American History were still entitled "Tentative Syllabi," and revisions of the 1987 edition, published before Sobol became commissioner, remained incomplete. While diversity had become a central part of a new rhetoric at the state level, the concept's actual impact on curricular programs was substantially less powerful than might have been expected. Opposition to reform ideas and attempts to mediate conflict impeded the construction of transformative concepts of American identity, but so too did the institutional priorities of social actors responsible for formulating policy.

## STRUGGLES OVER SEXUAL
## IDENTITY IN NEW YORK CITY

I now turn to a second case example of curricular reform in New York City to further illuminate obstacles to progressive change. In 1992 the city of New York designed a curriculum to teach respect and tolerance and to promote "mutual understanding among children who come to our schools from every corner of the world."[44] Its program, called *Children of the Rainbow*, encouraged the pursuit of a "global family," and "a world where all human beings are cherished for their inherent worth."[45]

As part of this agenda, designers of the Rainbow provided a section entitled "A Different Type of Family," which encouraged classroom teachers to enhance student awareness of diverse sexual orientations:

> Teachers of first graders have an opportunity to give children a healthy sense of identity at an early age. Classes should include references to lesbians/gay people in all curricular areas and should avoid exclusionary practices by presuming a person's sexual orientation, reinforcing stereotypes, or speaking of lesbians/gays as "they" or "other."[46]
>
> If teachers do not discuss lesbian/gay issues, they are not likely to come up. Children need actual experiences via creative play, books, visitors, etc. in order for them to view lesbians/gays as real people to be respected and appreciated. Educators have the potential to help increase the tolerance and acceptance of the lesbian/gay community and to decrease the staggering number of hate crimes perpetrated against them.[47]

In addition, the bibliography of the Rainbow's teaching guide listed several stories about gay or lesbian characters including the titles, *Daddy's Roommate*, *Gloria Goes to Gay Pride*, and *Heather Has Two Mommies*, a story "that describes a lesbian relationship and how one of the mommies is artificially inseminated."[48]

The *Rainbow* curriculum was in keeping with the state's commitment to teach multicultural education. *One Nation, Many Peoples* proposed to "help students to deal with human differences based upon linguistic diversity, gender, socioeconomic class, religion, sexual orientation, age, and the perspective and contributions of the physically challenged."[49] The inclusion of sexual orientation among the state's objectives marked a significant expansion in its effort to legitimate social differences and multiple identities as part of official knowledge. Though only a small part of the Rainbow curriculum, the initiative also signified a victory for gay and lesbian organizations that had been struggling for representation in the school curriculum for years. According to one account, when the school chancellor's advisory board discussed multicultural reforms in the late 1980s, "The board viewed culture as being connected to a people or a land or a country, and sexual orientation was not included as a culture."[50] After lengthy negotiations between Ecology (Educational Coalition on Lesbian and Gay Youth) and head of instruction for the board of education, Nilda Soto Ruiz, school officials hired Elissa Weindling, a member of the Gay and Lesbian Teachers Association, to design a section of the new first grade curriculum that would foster "positive attitudes toward sexuality."[51] Weindling wrote the passages cited earlier.

## A BACKLASH AGAINST
## PROGRESSIVE CHANGE

While proponents of sexual diversity in education believed it was an idea whose time had come, the Rainbow curriculum deeply polarized parents, religious groups, and social activists in New York City. By advising teachers to actively "initiate explorations of gay and lesbian issues in all classrooms since they [were] otherwise 'not likely to come up,'."[52] Weindling's proposals, critics claimed, crossed a line between giving some students material with which they could relate, and imposing on others "material about lives they are not experiencing."[53] When city officials issued the 443-page *Children of the Rainbow* curriculum in 1992, most of the city's thirty-two school districts simply chose to postpone discussion of homosexuality until the fifth or sixth grade.[54] But several other districts adamantly rejected parts of the curriculum,[55] and in November of 1992, Chancellor Joseph Fernandez suspended the school board in Queens because it refused to adopt any multicultural curriculum that included lessons of tolerance toward gay men and lesbians.[56]

Opponents of the Rainbow challenged the assertion that diverse sexual orientations and family arrangements were worthy of tolerance and positive recognition. Distinguishing between affirming racial and ethnic identities, which she deemed acceptable, and legitimizing sexual identities which she firmly rejected, District 24's president Mary Cummins declared, "we are going to continue to teach our students to appreciate the wide variety of religious traditions and racial and ethnic cultures represented in contemporary American society. . . . However we are not going to teach our children to treat all types of human behavior as equally safe, wholesome or acceptable."[57] Cummins was especially unwilling to accept the curriculum's portrayal of homosexual couples as families. Homosexual behaviors, according to Cummins, were immoralities against which students must be warned.[58]

Cummins' views revealed a critical difference between the public's familiarity with and acceptance of differences based on gender and race on the one hand and sexuality on the other. While the representation of women and minorities in official knowledge meant recognizing groups regarded, at least in theory, as equal, the inclusion of gays and lesbians would legitimate and validate a group whom Cummins and her supporters viewed as neither valid nor equal. From their perspective, attention to women and minorities was fair; by contrast, affirming gays and lesbians in school curricula posed a threat to their worldview. The issue of visibility is, of course, a significant part of gay politics. As sociologist Steven Seidman explains:

> Central to the gay liberation movements of the 1960s and 1970s was an affirmative politics of identity. If it was hard for women and people of color to find affirmative images of themselves and a forceful public voice, it was even harder for homosexuals. At least women and Blacks were a visible part of American culture. Blacks had fought in America's wars; there was a Black public culture that could offset mainstream racist images of personal inferiority. Women have been valued in their roles as wives, mothers, and social caretakers; twentieth century women could draw on women's rich cultural and political history. Homosexuals were invisible. They fought in wars, but no one knew; they were everywhere, but no one saw them. They were "closeted" or hid their identity for fear of losing their jobs and their families.[59]

Responding to the problem of invisibility, "Gay politics of the 1970s was organized around the affirmation of a lesbian and gay self. Gay knowledges reversed the cultural logic of the social mainstream: Homosexuality may have indicated a unique human type, but the homosexual, now transfigured into the 'lesbian' and 'gay man,' was the psychological, moral, and social equal to the heterosexual."[60]

This reversal creates a particular challenge for curricular reform in secondary schools because the inclusion of gays and lesbians cannot be accomplished with additive approaches commonly used to manage the treatment of different racial and ethnic groups. In the latter case, the visibility of women and racial minorities makes it possible to recognize these groups through a model of inclusion that values their sameness and incorporates them into the curriculum without disrupting mainstream assumptions, ideas, and values, and without questioning social norms or highlighting issues of discrimination. Hence, schools can and do acknowledge these groups and their cultural contributions by simply increasing the number of photographs of females or mentioning minority leaders and artists. By contrast, lacking visible markers, a gay inventor cannot "represent" the gay population without being identified as gay. Including gays and lesbians requires explaining who they are and making visible a politics that contests dominant norms and reverses the mainstream logic.

Indeed, the fact that no group contested the Rainbow curriculum's attention to diverse ethnic cultures reflects the success of additive approaches to presenting ethnic diversity. Having witnessed pressures for inclusion from racial and ethnic minorities since the 1960s, parents were prepared to see ethnic diversity in their children's school materials. But more significantly, they had little to resist; the curriculum addressed multiculturalism with very benign representations of ethnic differences. As one journalist aptly put it: "The bulk of *Children [of the Rainbow]* is songs and games intended to inoculate 6-year-olds against 'Eurocentrism' via plenty of *fun* exposure to other cultures. Thus there are directions for how to lead a class in playing African blindman's bluff, doing the Mexican hat dance, singing Irish ballads, baking Greek bread and making scrolls for the Chinese New Year."[61]

By contrast, criticisms of the Rainbow demonstrated first, that opponents did not view cultural and sexual diversity as one and the same, and second, that they especially resented the state's attempt to introduce sexual orientation into the curriculum as just another form of cultural diversity.

## THE BASES OF COMPETING VIEWS

The Rainbow curriculum split conservative Christians against gay rights activists; each side accused the other of imposing its beliefs on public schools.[62] But to fully understand the sources of conflict it is important to look at the bases of support and opposition and to situate reform ideas in a wider context of educational and social change.

To proponents of the Rainbow, the need to validate diverse sexual identities in the curriculum seemed self-evident; they defended inclusion as vital to education in the 1990s.[63] One advocate wrote, "The parents who protest the Rainbow curriculum grew up at a time when gay people were invisible. But their children will live in a different world."[64]

> Parents who attack the Rainbow curriculum aren't merely demanding the right to teach their own moral beliefs. They already have that right. They're demanding that competing ideas be silenced. They even want to banish facts—for example, that gay people lead happy, productive and satisfying lives. What kind of moral system is threatened by competing ideas and real-life facts?[65]

Like progressive petitioners in Texas, those who supported the curriculum's objectives saw knowledge about sexual orientation as critical to social change, to students' self-understanding, and to fostering students' respect for one another.

However, to opponents, curriculum reforms that promoted tolerance of homosexuality, condom distribution, and AIDS education expanded the school's domain too far beyond its traditional institutional functions. To poor and working class parents the inclusion of sexuality in the school curriculum symbolized the influence of professional upper-middle-class values on the state. Cummins portrayed the Rainbow as "part of the homosexual movement" and "gay and lesbian propaganda."[66] Like traditionalist petitioners in the Texas process who opposed progressive pedagogies because they challenged parental authority, Cummins argued that liberal-minded school officials were seeking to use an otherwise acceptable framework of cultural pluralism to undermine what was valued at home.[67] In a letter to 22,000 parents, Cummins condemned both *Children of the Rainbow* and AIDs education, thus linking knowledge about sexual identities to ongoing efforts to teach lessons about sexuality and sex education, and mobilizing parents around issues the Rainbow did not even address. Other opponents accused advocates not only of invading the family domain with unacceptable values, but also deceiving parents by slipping sexual orientation into the curriculum as a form of multicultural education.[68]

> "They want to teach my kid that being gay fits in with being Italian and Puerto Rican!" cried William Alfonso, a printer and father of three who said he supported the rest of the multicultural curriculum. "They snuck in a life style that has absolutely nothing to do with knowing each other and loving each other."[69]

Alfonso's response to curricular change echoes that of working class white parents who, in the face of shifting norms and the increasing visibility of social differences, have similarly targeted school knowledge at other points in time.[70] Sociologist Jonathan Rieder found that during the 1960s and 1970s, white working-class residents of the Brooklyn community of Canarsie who withdrew their traditional support for liberal ideas were responding to not only a loss of moral and cultural anchors, but also a loss of authority to the media, the culture industry,[71] and the professional sector.[72]

By the 1990s, some opponents of the Rainbow charged that new curricular reforms were prioritizing social issues over traditional educational functions. A member of the Family Defense Council declared, " 'Children should be your priority, not a gay agenda, not multiculturalism or multi-sexualism. That has nothing to do with education.' "[73]

Likewise, members of New York City's Central Board of Education complained that Chancellor Fernandez had focused too much attention on controversial social agendas while neglecting low test scores and poor conditions in the city's schools. According to the received dogma of the therapeutic culture, children had rights to self-fulfillment, affirmation, and empowerment, and schools now had a responsibility to support and protect these rights, to nurture student identities, and to foster pride, while becoming active agents in the fight against prejudice, harassment, AIDS, teenage pregnancies, and teenage suicides. Fernandez readily acknowledged that he supported the Rainbow curriculum because he believed these subjects were educationally relevant.

> A lot of people call this a social agenda that's irrelevant to the three R's. . . . But I think it's the fourth R—respect for yourself and others. In the first place, schools have to teach things that, for one reason or another, aren't getting taught elsewhere. For instance, people's fathers used to teach them to drive, but now you learn this in school, because who has time to teach driving? And schools have always taught values—"civics" is the old word—because only mutual tolerance allows us to keep the first three R's on the front burner. And if we're truly here for all children, then we have to keep faith with them, whatever their situation at any given moment—perhaps they're pregnant, or they're confused about who they are, or they're substance abusers. Ultimately, when history is written, this administration will be shown to have saved lives, to have mended lives.[74]

However, to those who rejected the aims of the Rainbow, the role of schools in performing these functions was by no means so obvious. Debates over the new curriculum afforded an opportunity to clarify the purpose of education rather than to expand its domain.

## THE IMPACT OF RESISTANCE

Despite Fernandez's strong convictions, by late January of 1993, resistance to the curriculum pressured him to make concessions that diluted the curriculum's capacity to enhance the visibility of homosexual identities. Fernandez accepted curricular revisions that "toned down the document so that most references to 'lesbian/gay families' were replaced with the phrase 'same gender couples.' "[75] Responding to concerns about the curriculum's accessibility to first graders, curriculum planners replaced the term "lesbian" with the notion of "having two mommies at home." The book *Heather Has Two Mommies* was eliminated from bibliographic references as inappropriate for first graders, while "other books on gay and lesbian families, including *Daddy's Roommate* would be added."[76] Fernandez also chose to exclude the program's suggestion that "Classes should include references to lesbians/gay people in all curricular areas."[77]

What had begun as a seemingly powerful official affirmation of diverse sexual orientations became a weaker attempt to acknowledge different family relations without explicitly recognizing sexual identities. Resistance in this case substantially modified a potentially transformative idea, and despite his concessions, Fernandez's support for progressive curricular reforms had high political stakes. In contrast to decision makers in Texas's textbook adoption system who were insulated from public mobilizations by their professional roles in a formal institutional process, Fernandez's position proved more vulnerable. The city's central board denied him a new contract as school chancellor after representatives from Queens, Staten Island, Brooklyn, and the Bronx voted four to three against him.

## CURRICULAR STRUGGLE IN PERSPECTIVE

While public mobilizations impeded the realization of curricular goals in New York City, the long-term significance of cultural battles was less clear. School board elections in May of 1993 underscored the persistence and intensity of feelings for and against the new model of pluralism as parents reiterated their conflicting views. Rita Eagen, a sixty-year-old resident of Queens explained, "I want to give my vote to those who represent the right way of life. . . . It's not right for our children to be exposed to the gay and lesbian issue at such a young age. They should learn about the issue on their own, when they are a little older."[78] In contrast, a mother from Park Slope in Brooklyn said, "We need to teach tolerance. . . . We have to accept the fact that we're all living here together . . . . Sex is everywhere," she said. "To think that kids aren't going to learn about sex outside the school is absurd. It's important that they get correct information about sex and AIDS."[79] Journalists described election campaigns as the "broadest effort since 1970 to use school elections to assert control over the curriculum."[80] Conservative candidates backed by the Roman Catholic Archdiocese of New York, Pat Robertson's Christian Coalition, and Concerned Parents for Educational Accountability competed against candidates favored by gay advocacy groups and Protestant and Jewish clergy for 288 seats. In his run for reelection, then Mayor David Dinkins urged a large voter turnout to prevent the election of conservative school board candidates.

Yet, given forecasts about widespread community interest, actual participation in the school board elections was surprisingly low.[81] In 1993 voter turnout was 9 percent, higher than the 7-percent turnout of the previous year, but less than the 14-percent turnout in 1970 when decentralization was a primary issue. Although voters did elect numerous new school board members, little ideological change occurred overall. Some candidates who shared the views of the Christian Coalition won school board seats, but so too did members with more moderate views. Conservative districts remained conservative while traditionally liberal districts became somewhat more liberal as candidates backed by gay and liberal alliances also won seats.

Meanwhile, despite the heated conflicts over curriculum reforms and strong preelection attention to school board candidates' curricular views, concern about the curriculum seemed to dissipate after the elections. One school principal noted that practical obstacles restricted the curriculum's actual impact on what was taught. She informed a journalist that "the whole debate had always been a non-issue. There had been so many retirements among principals this year that most schools in her district, at least, never even got copies of the teachers' guides for the Rainbow curriculum—so they were in no position either to use it or to reject it."[82] Three years later, Delco Cornett, a board member in District 2, also emphasized the realities of curricular implementation over time. "No parent has complained to me about someone doing something inappropriate in the classroom," he said. "Ultimately, I think the teachers have common sense, and they don't seem to go overboard."[83] Both comments reinforce one former teacher's earlier statement to a *New York Times* reporter.

> "With all these titans battling up there, it may not matter who wins or loses," Mr. Fager said. "There's an enormous gap between 110 Livingston, which could be on the moon, and the schools. It's one thing to order a district to use it [a curriculum], but it's another thing for teachers to actually use it."[84]

These observations provide a segue to the question of what curricular debates mean in terms of everyday classroom practice. Regardless of whose perspectives they advance, curricular policies matter little unless schoolteachers, who are most responsible for transmitting knowledge, implement them. While cultural and political struggles come and go, the institutional realization of curricular goals depends upon teachers' perspectives and behaviors.

Despite conflicting beliefs about culture and pedagogy, scholars at the state level and activists in New York City shared a common understanding of school knowledge as a medium of values and beliefs. Like petitioners in Texas, whether participants in curricular struggles sought to recognize one history or many histories, one culture or many cultures, they treated school knowledge as an embodiment of social interests and worldviews, and they praised or feared its capacity to mold students into obedient or rebellious citizens. In contrast, teachers in New York City, like teachers in Texas, viewed curricular policies in a very different way. How they respond to curricular mandates and what matters to them are the subject of the next chapter.

## NOTES

1. New York State Social Studies Review and Development Committee, *One Nation, Many Peoples: A Declaration of Cultural Interdependence* (New York: New York State Education Department, 1991), vi.

2. The report provided the foundation for Sobol's eventual curricular plan called "Understanding Diversity."

3. New York State, *One Nation, Many Peoples*, xi.

4. New York State, *One Nation, Many Peoples*, 9.

5. David Nasaw, *Schooled to Order* (New York: Oxford University Press, 1979), 40.

6. Henry A. Giroux, "Schooling as a Form of Cultural Politics: Toward a Pedagogy of and for Difference," in *Critical Pedagogy, the State, and Cultural Struggle*, ed. Henry A. Giroux and Peter McLaren (Albany, N.Y.: SUNY Press, 1989), 143–44. Giroux advances a theory of critical pedagogy that makes students active participants in the learning process; their experiences and identities are key to their own empowerment (see Giroux, "Schooling as Cultural Politics," 149).

7. Steven D. Houser, social studies chairman at Horace Greeley High School in Chappaqua, N.Y., quoted in Joseph Berger, "New Diversity Old Hat in Some Schools," *New York Times*, 22 June 1991, sec. I, p. 26.

8. Jeffrey Perchuk, Midwood High School in Brooklyn, quoted in Berger, "New Diversity Old Hat," sec. I, p. 26.

9. Kevin Sack, "Cuomo Wary of Revisions in Curriculum," *New York Times*, 16 July 1991, sec. B, p. 4.

10. New York State, *One Nation, Many Peoples*, 39.

11. New York State, *One Nation, Many Peoples*, 39.

12. Catherine Cornbleth and Dexter Waugh, *The Great Speckled Bird* (New York: St. Martin's, 1995), 99.

13. New York State, *One Nation, Many Peoples*, 45.

14. New York State, *One Nation, Many Peoples*, 46.

15. Nathan Glazer, quoted in New York State, *One Nation, Many Peoples*, 35.

16. New York State, *One Nation, Many Peoples*, 35–36.

17. K. Anthony Appiah, "Identity, Authenticity, Survival: Multicultural Socie-ties and Social Reproduction," in *Multiculturalism*, ed. Charles Taylor and Amy Gutmann (Princeton, N.J.: Princeton University Press, 1994), 162–63.

18. Cornbleth and Waugh, *Great Speckled Bird,* 119.

19. Cornbleth and Waugh, *Great Speckled Bird*, 118. The authors note that the social studies review committee deliberated over three themes: "(1) supporting teachers in making desired changes, (2) whether and how to address African-American experience and racism in the United States, and (3) the nature and emphasis to place on a common or shared American culture."

20. Cornbleth and Waugh, *Great Speckled Bird*, 110.

21. Cornbleth and Waugh, *Great Speckled Bird*, 112–13.

22. Thomas Sobol, memo to the Honorable Members of the Board of Regents, State Education Department/University of the State of New York, 12 July 1991, Albany, 5.

23. Sobol, memo, 6.

24. Sobol, memo, 7

25. Sobol, memo, 8.

26. Sobol, memo, 9–10.

27. New York State, *One Nation, Many Peoples*, 35.

28. Sobol, memo, 12.

29. Sam Howe Verhovek, "Way Cleared for Changes in Curriculum," *New York Times*, 26 July 1991, sec. B, p. 1.

30. Cornbleth and Waugh, *Great Speckled Bird*, 135.

31. Cornbleth and Waugh, *Great Speckled Bird*, 141. The authors document the particular compromises that were made on pp. 139–41.

32. Cornbleth and Waugh, *Great Speckled Bird*, 141.

33. Cornbleth and Waugh, *Great Speckled Bird*, 142.

34. Sam Howe Verhovek, "Plan to Emphasize Minority Cultures Ignites a Debate," *New York Times*, 21 June 1991, sec. A, p. 1.

35. Martin Carnoy, "Education, State, and Culture in American Society," in *Critical Pedagogy, the State, and Cultural Struggle*, ed. Henry Giroux and Peter Mc-Laren (Albany, N.Y.: SUNY Press, 1989), 4.

36. Michael W. Apple, *Official Knowledge* (New York: Routledge, 1993), 78.

37. New York State, *One Nation, Many Peoples*, 18.

38. New York State, *One Nation, Many Peoples*, 20.

39. New York State, *One Nation, Many Peoples*, 20.

40. Ruth Sidel, *Battling Bias: The Struggle for Identity and Community on College Campuses* (New York: Penguin, 1994), 10–11. The difference between identity as an individual characteristic and identity as a reflection of social relations is captured in Sidel's description of adolescent identities. She writes: "Whereas many Ameri-cans think of identity in purely individual, psychological terms, in reality our iden-tity, both in the eyes of others and in our own eyes, is an intricate web of our particular individual characteristics and our place in the social and economic hierar-chies of our society."

41. Catherine O'Leary, "Education Reform as Cultural Critique: The Knowl-edge/Power Boundary of Liberal Political Identity," Paper delivered at the 1995

Annual Meeting of the American Political Science Association, Chicago, August 31–September 3, 1–23. In a comparative analysis of *One Nation, Many Peoples* and its more controversial predecessor, *A Curriculum of Inclusion*, O'Leary argues that the former reinforces a liberal nationalist paradigm while the latter "questioned the terms on which 'other' cultures are represented in the curriculum," 5. *A Curriculum of Inclusion* was a 1989 report by the Task Force on Minorities: Equity and Excellence. See Sam Howe Verhovek, "New York Education Chief Seeks New Stress on Nonwhite Cultures," *New York Times*, 7 February 1990, sec. A, p. 1, 4. The report asserted that "African-Americans, Asian-Americans, Puerto Ricans/Latinos, and native Americans have all been the victims of an intellectual and educational oppression that has characterized the culture and institutions of the United States." See Sobol, memo, 2. The committee proposed that state syllabi include "more of the experience of Black, Latino, Asian, Native American and other groups which constitute significant minorities in American society." Also see Edward B. Fiske, "Lessons," *New York Times*, 7 February 1990, sec. B, p. 5. *A Curriculum of Inclusion* urged the state to change the curriculum "so that minority students 'will have higher self-esteem and self-respect, while children from European cultures will have a less arrogant perspective.' " Fiske also quotes Bill Honig, California's superintendent of public instruction, who called the report "nothing but racism." See Diane Ravitch, "Diversity and Tradition," Letters to the Editor, *New York Times*, 28 February 1990, sec. A, p. 26. She notes that the report provoked immediate and intense criticism for its "anti-white and anti-Western rhetoric."

42. Cornbleth and Waugh, *Great Speckled Bird*, 145.

43. Cornbleth and Waugh, *Great Speckled Bird*, 149.

44. New York City Board of Education, *Children of the Rainbow* (New York: Board of Education of the City of New York, 1990), iii.

45. New York City Board of Education, *Children of the Rainbow*, iii.

46. Steven Lee Myers, "School Board in Queens Shuns Fernandez Meeting," *New York Times*, 3 December 1992, sec. B, p. 3.

47. Myers, "School Board in Queens," sec. B, p. 3.

48. "Rainbow, Revised," editorial in *New York Times*, 30 June 1993, sec. I, p. 20.

49. New York State, *One Nation, Many Peoples*, 9.

50. Sheila Evans-Tranumn, chairwoman of the board and a member of the New York Alliance of Black Educators, quoted in Josh Barbanel, "Under 'Rainbow,' a War: When Politics, Morals, and Learning Mix," *New York Times*, 27 December 1992, sec. I, p. 34.

51. Barbanel, "Under 'Rainbow,' a War," sec. I, p. 34.

52. Barbanel, "Under 'Rainbow,' a War," sec. I, p. 34.

53. Sydney Schwartz, professor of early childhood education, quoted in Barbanel, "Under 'Rainbow,' a War," sec. I, p. 34.

54. "School Board's Confusing Signals," editorial in *New York Times*, 12 December 1992, sec. I, p. 22. By December 12, eight districts had adopted the guide without making changes, seventeen were working out compromises and revisions, and six were discussing alterations.

55. See Mary B. W. Tabor, "S.I. Drops Gay Issues from Student Guide, *New*

*York Times*, June 1992, Sec. B, p. 3. By June, District 20 in Brooklyn had "objected to references to gay and lesbian households and banned sections of the curriculum," and District 18, composed of East Flatbush and Canarsie in Brooklyn, had rejected "sections of the curriculum, in part because teachers had not been offered training sessions on how to address questions about lesbian and gay families." Likewise, the community school board of West Brighton, District 31 in Staten Island, "voted 7 to 0, with one abstention" to delete "the section of the curriculum [that] talks about gay and lesbian parents and includes bibliographical entries related to that topic." See Steven Lee Myers, "Values in Conflict," *New York Times*, 6 October 1992, sec. B, p. 6. Districts 31, 20, 8, and 12 ultimately "voted to reject only those pages dealing with gay men and lesbians" rather than the entire curriculum.

56. Steven Lee Myers, "Queens School Board Suspended in Fight on Gay-Life Curriculum," *New York Times*, 2 December 1992, sec. A, p. 1. Myers reports it was the first time in New York City's twenty-two-year history of decentralization that its chancellor suspended a local school board over a curricular issue and the first time in Fernandez's three years in office that he had suspended an entire board for any reason.

57. Stephanie Gutmann, "The Curriculum That Ate New York," in *Insight on the News* 9 (15 March 1993): 8.

58. Myers, "Values in Conflict," sec. B, p. 1. One parent said, "I don't think you should teach innocent children that's [homosexuality] an acceptable life style. . . . You should teach them the normal one, the old-fashioned one, white picket fences and a mommy and a daddy."

59. Steven Seidman, *Contested Knowledge* (Cambridge, Mass.: Blackwell, 1994), 263.

60. Seidman, *Contested Knowledge*, 263.

61. Gutmann, "Curriculum That Ate New York," 7.

62. Joseph Berger, "A Mix of Earlier Skirmishes Converges in the Rainbow Curriculum Battle," *New York Times*, 3 December 1992, sec. B, p. 4.

63. Christopher Bauer, a resident of Staten Island and a member of then Mayor David Dinkins's Police Council of Lesbian and Gay Issues, said "Children of lesbian and gay families generally start school in the first grade like everyone else. . . . How are these children supposed to feel as they advance through the school system until they reach a grade that is 'age appropriate'?" Quoted in Tabor, "S.I. Drops Gay Issues," sec. B, p. 3.

64. Sasha Alyson, "Fear of the Rainbow," *New York Times*, 30 December 1992, sec. A, p. 15. Alyson is founder and editor of Alyson Wonderland that publishes children's books about families with lesbian and gay parents, several of which were mentioned in the first version of the curriculum guide.

65. Alyson, "Fear of the Rainbow," sec. A, p. 15.

66. Barbanel, "Under 'Rainbow,' a War," sec. I, p. 34. See Myers, "Values in Conflict," sec. B, p. 6.

67. See Sam Roberts, "In Brooklyn's District 15, Divisions of the City Are Reflected in the Campaign," *New York Times*, 2 May 1993, sec. I, p. 49. Roberts observed that the debate "reflected divisions between advocates of so-called back-to-basics schooling and those favoring innovative teaching styles; between what are

perceived as working-class and middle-class values over the role of schools as surrogate parents in dispensing sex education and condoms; and between often liberal whites and often conservative Hispanic people."

68. See Tony Hiss, "The End of the Rainbow," *New Yorker*, 12 April 1993, 50. Hiss wrote: "Parents, including those who don't care if their kids ever go to college, generally take an intense and very protective interest in what happens during the first years of school; for many who spoke against Fernandez at the hearing, each successive action of his had been more threatening than the one before: the man had targeted first teen-agers, then ten-year-olds, and, finally, children who were only six. These people said that the chancellor had abandoned them and then turned on them. In their view, talking about sex in schools, even when the intent of such talk is to save lives or to move beyond hatred, is a direct invasion of their own homes, even their bedrooms."

69. Quoted in Tabor, "S.I. Drops Gay Issues," sec. B, p. 3.

70. Lillian Rubin described working-class parents of the late 1970s and early 80s as "feeling helplessly out of control" in the midst of economic and cultural change. See Rubin, *Families on the Fault Line* (New York: HarperCollins 1994, 63). "They yearn for a past when, it seems to them, moral absolutes reigned, yet they're confused and uncertain about which of yesterday's moral strictures they want to impose on themselves and their children today. Rubin found that new immigrants, nonwhite groups, and the policies of multicultural education and affirmative action that are believed to serve their interests, became a convenient target of blame for working-class parents seeking to understand their economic woes as well as their sense of moral confusion and disunity. "As whites they have been the dominant group, the favored ones, the ones who could count on getting the job when people of color could not. Now suddenly there are others—not just individual others but identifiable groups, people who share a history, a language, a culture, even a color—who lay claim to some of the rights and privileges that formerly had been labeled 'for whites only.' And whites react as if they've been betrayed, as if a sacred promise has been broken. They're white, aren't they? They're real Americans, aren't they? This is their country, isn't it?" (187). Also see Myers, "Values in Conflict," sec. B, p. 6. Myers notes that the Rainbow controversy occurred in one of the city's "most ethnically diverse and overcrowded school districts with 27,000 students—49 percent of whom are Hispanic, 27 percent white, 18 percent Asian, and 6 percent black. . . . The controversy over 'Children of the Rainbow' has unfolded in a district with the very sort of ethnic diversity the curriculum was meant to celebrate. The district takes in a wide, mostly working-class swath of western Queens, including Maspeth, Ridgewood, Middle Village, Glendale, Elmhurst and Corona. The district's southern part is mostly white and a stronghold of Queens conservatism, while the northern part has seen an enormous influx of immigrants."

71. Jonathan Rieder, *Canarsie* (Cambridge, Mass.: Harvard University Press, 1985), 142. Rieder writes: "Everywhere they looked, it seemed that the sentries of the culture had relaxed their vigilance. People no longer observed the taboos that once had functioned as voluntary forms of moral coordination. The intrusive powers of law, popular culture, the schools, and news media exposed family space to moral dangers as surely as racial change exposed physical space to physical dangers.

The confessional frankness of modern television was not simply upsetting in itself; it contributed to the loosening of parents' ability to 'bring their kids up right.' As one Italian father put it: 'I think they are giving wrong ideas to children of today who look on these programs, because these people like Johnny Carson or David Susskind or Merv Griffin say these things about people living together or homosexuals, and the children believe these people are men who know what they're talking about and if they talk about it nonchalantly, then the kids think there shouldn't be anything wrong with it. By not saying anything, by not condemning it, they are sort of putting an okay on it.' "

72. Rieder, *Canarsie*, 145. An Italian policeman observed, "Parents today tell the kid, 'You got your rights,' and one of our big [New York State] Regents professors said, 'Shouldn't children in elementary schools have their rights?' Oh no, I disagree with this, can you imagine a ten-year-old, an eleven-year-old, a twelve-year-old with rights? They got no rights. Their right is me. I am the parent, I will be his right, I will decide what is right or wrong for them!"

73. Carol Wood quoted in Peter Marks, "Fernandez Silently Sits in Real-Life People's Court," *New York Times*, 11 February 1993, sec. B, p. 2.

74. Hiss, "End of the Rainbow," 46.

75. Josh Barbanel, "Fernandez Modifies Parts of Curriculum about Gay Parents," *New York Times*, 27 January 1993, sec. A, p. 1.

76. Barbanel, "Fernandez Modifies Parts of Curriculum," sec. B, p. 3.

77. Gutmann, "Curriculum That Ate New York," 10.

78. Sam Dillon, "After Moral Debate, Voters Shape Schools' Future," *New York Times*, 5 May 1993, sec. B, p. 4.

79. Dillon, "After Moral Debate," sec. B, p. 4.

80. Sam Dillon, "Curriculum Issues Fuel Races for School Boards," *New York Times*, 24 March 1993, sec. B, p. 1.

81. See Sam Dillon, "Voters Show Increased Interest in School Elections," *New York Times*, 4 May 1993, sec. B, p. 8, for analysis of why school board elections garnered so much attention.

82. Hiss, "End of the Rainbow," 47.

83. Pam Belluck, "Conservative School Board Gains Turned Out to Be No Revolution," *New York Times*, 29 April 1996, sec. B, p. 2.

84. Steven Lee Myers, "Few Using Curriculum in Dispute," *New York Times*, 6 December 1992, sec. I, p. 53.

*5*

# Implementing New Ideas: Classroom Realities in New York

It is 8:30 on a Tuesday morning and I am standing on the steps of a New York City High School amid a mass of young people waiting to begin their school day. I feel small, not only because many of the students are taller than I, but also because there are so very many of them. It is taking a surprisingly long time to filter through the three sets of open doors at the front entrance of the building, and I am beginning to worry that I will be late for my interview. By contrast, the students seem remarkably patient. I soon learn that their wait is part of a daily routine. On the other side of the doors, their peers are placing their schoolbags on conveyer belts similar to those at metropolitan airports and walking through metal detectors monitored by two security officers. To the left of the metal detectors is a third security guard who is busy directing late students to a side desk where they must secure a late pass. I am struck by the number of late students who are sauntering in. Tardiness appears to be routine too.

As a visitor, I give my name to an attendant at the reception desk who calls upstairs to Betty Walters, one of thirty New York City high school teachers I interviewed.[1] Moments later Betty introduces herself and leads me through a crowded, bustling corridor. The school has five thousand students she informs me as we search for a quiet place to talk. This turns out to be no easy task. Walters does not have her own class-room and the teachers' lounge is already occupied. Eventually, we end up in the office of the assistant principal who offers us his space for the period. We would later need to move to a different site.

Walters' school is typical of many I visited—quite concerned about safety and seriously overcrowded. Students and teachers come and go in shifts; like Walters, many teachers move from classroom to classroom in the course of a day. As another teacher I interviewed explained, the lack of stability at his school makes it difficult to accomplish basic instructional tasks.

> I gotta walk around and carry my own maps because if I leave a map behind in the classroom, it's going to disappear. I'm a gypsy. I teach in three different classrooms. I would love to have my own room, stockpile all my things in my room. But I'm not carrying books and papers and maps and everything around the building. My building is crowded. My building is designed for 2,300 students; we have 3,300. Passing is like riding a subway during rush hour, it's crazy. There's a limit to what I can do, and it's very very very frustrating.

Others mentioned having little or no access to basic supplies, photocopiers, and video equipment. I describe the physical and material conditions of these schools because they are part of the institutional and organizational frameworks that structure how teachers work and how they teach the curriculum. More significantly, they are one of the factors that influence whether teachers teach the curriculum at all.

## CURRICULAR POLICY AT THE CLASSROOM LEVEL

New York's curriculum plan, *One Nation, Many Peoples*, positioned teachers to play a key role in implementing multicultural reforms. Teachers, curriculum planners proposed, would "develop their students' capacities to take multiple perspectives"[2] and "incorporate a range of interactive modes of teaching and learning in order to foster understanding . . . examination of controversy, and mutual learning."[3] These goals are consistent with reconstructive educational visions. Theorists Stanely Aronowitz and Henry Giroux, for example, view teachers as "transformative intellectuals"[4] who are dedicated "to the values of the intellect and the enhancement of the critical powers of the young."[5] By providing a critical pedagogy that "problematizes knowledge, utilizes dialogue, and makes knowledge meaningful, critical, and ultimately emancipatory," teachers, they suggest, can create "the conditions for students to be able to speak, write, and assert critically their own histories, voices, and learning experiences."[6]

Because teachers mediate the relationship between curricular policies and what students are taught, their views and behaviors are central to explaining whether and how official knowledge actually becomes school knowledge. Following Pierre Bourdieu, if knowledge is not inherently worthy, then the question is not whether social and institutional forces determine its value but *how* do they determine it?[7] How does education "refract(s) external demands into its own logic"?[8] How do new ideas become "institutionally shared beliefs?"[9] What happens when they do? If teachers are to carry out radical progressive reforms, we would expect them to feel empowered by their positions as educators and intellectuals, committed or at least attuned to the aims of new agendas, and confident about their capacity to stimulate a critical consciousness among their students.

However, while listening to teachers talk about their work, I learned that they do not usually feel this way and it is in fact very difficult for them to carry out new projects. Alternative curricular ideas are not received in a vacuum, nor are they implemented in contexts devoid of long-standing organizational and social practices that are especially entrenched in public schools. In fact, as new or recycled concepts *become* institutionalized beliefs, they are integrated into an established system of norms, routines, and often unquestioned logic that govern whether and how they are incorporated. Once policies are contextualized, they are viewed through a lens already colored by assumptions about how things are done or must be done. Thus, in addition to the physical and material conditions previously described, particular social experiences, mental frameworks, and paradigms shape how curricular ideas are received and structure how teachers feel about and do their work.

The Texas textbook adoption process showed that a logic of technocratic rationality undermined teachers' capacity to participate in producing and evaluating educational content.[10] According to this logic, "the form that school knowledge takes and the pedagogy used to legitimate it become subordinated to principles of efficiency, hierarchy, and control."[11] Likewise, narratives from my sample of New York City teachers revealed how these principles affected not only their ability to put policies into practice, but also how they treated curricular issues vis-à-vis other concerns related to their jobs. In light of the controversies *One Nation, Many Peoples* sparked among academic scholars, I expected those whom I interviewed to be both interested in and knowledgeable about state efforts to encourage diversity in the curriculum. But surprisingly, only two had heard of the report; even more, those unfamiliar with it were quite blasé about not knowing. In fact, after briefly addressing my questions about curricular change in the first few minutes of conversation, most respondents moved swiftly and with much more animation to other issues. Had I not persisted in revisiting the topic of curriculum, I do not believe the subject would have come up again.

The themes that emerged in teachers' accounts illuminate how they interpret and respond to curricular policies in general, and to policies encouraging diversity in particular. I argue that at the level of classroom practice—what teachers teach and how they teach—their potential to implement curricular reforms is substantially moderated by the physical and material conditions of their work, as well as the external requirements they are expected to meet, their individual perspectives on diversity and curricular reform, and their perceptions of students' characteristics and abilities. I then suggest that the gap between reforms and classroom practice is likely to be reduced not by focusing exclusively on teachers' attitudes, biases, and limitations, but by establishing a dialogue with teachers that acknowledges and addresses the realities of their work.

## TEACHING IN AN URBAN HIGH SCHOOL

Many teachers described feeling disempowered by a large bureaucracy over which they have very little control. When asked to describe how they plan their courses, teachers universally cited the New York State Regents Exam as having the most influence on what they teach. Their students must pass the regents exams to gain admission to college and the Regents Competency Tests (RCT) in U.S. history and government to receive a high school diploma. Schools give exams in June; teachers typically spend the last several weeks of the semester preparing students for them. Because local and state officials use exam scores to measure not only students' performance, but also that of schools and teachers, teachers treat the regents exams, rather than curricular policies such as *One Nation, Many Peoples* as the most important source of official knowledge. Anne Thompson, who has been teaching for fifteen years, summarized the impact of exams on teaching this way: "What drives the curriculum? I hate to tell you, what drives the curriculum is the Regents. And I find we teach too much to the Regents. We don't teach for understanding, we teach for the Regents." In this way, external prescriptions of what knowledge counts tightly structure the course of each semester.

But while curriculum reforms increase teachers' responsibilities, they diminish their authority to decide what to teach. Describing themselves as "those of us in the trenches" and decision makers in more abstract, impersonal terms—the powers that be, on high, those in Albany, the Board of Ed, 110 Livingston Street—teachers such as Tony Rosario felt as if state authorities mandated policies without notice or explanation, and certainly without dialogue.

> We don't even know decisions are in the works until we find out that they've been already made. And then we're handed, I don't know, anywhere from a hundred to five hundred page memo telling us that this has been decided. This is the way it's going to happen. There's always an incubation period, it won't start 'til next June or next this or next that. Then, there's no training. There's nobody to explain anything to you. We call our board of ed; it's like the biggest bureaucracy in the world. You can't get anyone to answer you. They're very unfriendly. . . . And you say to yourself, why did you ever, ever join the educational system when they don't have any inclination of helping students? I mean, if I'm calling the board of ed, I'm not calling for myself.

The absence of communication between policy makers and teachers reinforces the latter's perceptions that administrators and policy makers have little respect or need for their input. Greg Galiano explained how the lack of respect and understanding from supervisors and the state affects teachers' identities.

> We don't identify ourselves as real professionals. We don't. We just don't. And I know we are. I believe we are, but if I want to go to a meeting, [I hear] "oh, you've been on too many trips this year." I've been on one trip. Or, "you've been on too many trips; you need to be in the classroom." But you're not motivating me, the person who's responsible for really making that lesson good.

A diminished professional identity contributes to a sense of cynicism and a propensity to defy the system. When discussing the topic of curricular policy, for example, teachers react with indifference at best, and in some cases, with more than a tinge of hostility. Arguing that curricular agendas and in-service training were a waste of his time, David Thompson, a Staten Island teacher, remarked:

> The general feeling [about multicultural education] among teachers is very negative, o.k.? Because essentially . . . I don't think that multicultural education has been articulated very well. I have not read those works, and most teachers do not. And we're not interested in reading that kind of stuff. And there very much is an attitude among teachers of, we go to these meetings, and people get up and talk to us about the way that things are going to be "different." And we just, like, doodle on a piece of paper. It goes in one ear and out the other. You know, I do my class and I shut the door, and I do whatever the hell I want. Now, does that mean that I'm supposed to be teaching about India, and I'm teaching about Viking II landing on Mars? No. Within the constraints of the curriculum I do teach that [about India].

George Kostas claimed that he rarely used the curriculum, opting instead to act upon his gut feelings of what motivates his students.

> If you accept that a teacher is someone who does his magic show, that every fifteen seconds keeps kids going, I'm sure I do many of the wrong things. As the five years have gone by, I've developed some skills which I guess are teacher skills which have made me a little better at trying to keep the kids interested. But I can assure you that I *never* use the curriculum.
>
> So, no matter what it the curriculum says to us, the curriculum I have somewhere, we basically, I basically, I can't say what other people do, try to keep the kids interested, try to keep them involved with what's going on in the world, and so I ask questions. So, I don't care what the curriculum says. I don't teach them dates, I don't teach them history. I teach them reasons and relationships. Now, sometimes that's in fad; sometimes it's out of fad.

Kostas' notion of educational fads effectively captures how many teachers assess the life expectancy of new curricular ideas. Because state and local officials are continually attempting to revise the curriculum, and reform agendas slip so quickly in and out of fashion, teachers feel it is futile to treat any of them very seriously. Expecting that most ideas will be short lived, some dismiss them reflexively as meaningless buzzwords; cooperative education, portfolio assessment, and multiple intelligences are among the many concepts that have come and gone. The specific idea did not seem to matter. Teachers were consistently skeptical of the value of each simply because they perceived these ideas to be out of sync with the realities of classroom teaching and their attempts to develop meaningful lesson plans.

Even further removed from the daily realities of teaching, academic theories of education and curriculum carried little weight as well. Hannah Rose advised, "Forget about the *Harvard Educational Review.*"

> *The Harvard Educational Review* has very little to do with New York City. . . . It's bull shit. I mean, it is great if you have a small number of kids, and resources. Think of me. I'm about five feet tall. I have tenth grade classes of 48, 45, 46, 39 [students] in honors. Think that two-thirds of these kids [the other kids in the high school] have failed ninth grade. All right. Now you tell me about all those wonderful things. I had kids taking tests leaning on two-drawer file cabinets. I had another kid using a music stand as a desk. Do I need to go on?

Renee Kelley, who was planning to leave the teaching profession, affirmed Rose's point. Policy makers and theorists have no shortage of fancy concepts, but seem oblivious to those who will bear the task of translating ill-formed ideas into practice. They show little evidence of ever having stood in teachers' shoes. As she put it, "Yes, it would be great to discover universal truths about justice and liberty and inequality, but you know, we're busy trying to define the word 'constitution.' " Steven Bernstein concurred, "The curriculum is not even secondary, it's tertiary. It just doesn't mean anything when you have everything else in the way." Despite differences in years and range of experience, teachers almost uniformly emphasized the rate and means by which new policies are promoted, their lack of participation in curriculum planning, and a gulf between policy expectations and the material, social, and organizational challenges of classroom practice.

## THE MEANING OF
## MULTICULTURAL EDUCATION

If teachers are dubious of curricular change in general, how do they regard particular initiatives to teach diversity? For most of the teachers I interviewed, the need for New York State's multicultural reforms was by no means obvious. When I asked whether multicultural education has influenced the teaching of social studies, teachers' responses indicated a rather narrow understanding of the concept. Upon hearing the term "multicultural education," most referred immediately to the teaching of global studies. A two-semester sequence, global studies includes the study of Latin America, Asia, Africa, and Western Europe, and no one contested its inclusion in the curriculum or questioned the value of learning about different cultures within the global studies framework.

By contrast, teachers were less receptive to using multicultural approaches to teach U.S. history. Their rationales ranged from the notion that multicultural education hardly differed from what they had been teaching all along to more critical assessments of multiculturalism's limitations and costs. Bernstein, for example, said that the emphasis on inclusion created a practical dilemma by expanding an already overwhelming task; teachers now feel pressured to cover not only colonial America, the Civil War, and other traditionally valued topics, but also the experiences of different groups.

> This multiculturalism. I call it "multi-culty," it's meaningless. It's degenerated into ethnic cheerleading. Some people feel that you're going to hurt the feelings of any particular group of students if you don't take into account their ethnicity, their national origin, or their religious background. Now, I don't want a classroom that's homogeneous. I don't live in a homogeneous society.

I like my school because we have so many different students from so many
different parts of the world. But not all subjects are going to be treated equally.
I have in my classroom this year two children who are Thai. Does that mean
that I have to give them, or create special lessons, "Thais in American history"
. . . I'm not going to denigrate anybody's culture, I'm not going to denigrate
anybody's history, but simply because you are in my class does not automati-
cally guarantee that there's something to be said [about your culture].

History teacher Thompson pointed out that textbook efforts to
address diversity were glaringly tokenistic.

This is a brand new textbook, and you can see from the cover . . . it's aiming
at multiculturalism. You're either Chinese, you're Ancient Greek and you're
African. And the kids realize this, we just got this the other day. The textbook
we'd been using had an Egyptian statue, an Egyptian on the front, and Greek
on the back. And I hand these out to the kids and I say "I'd like you to take a
look at the cover, what is the message?" And they all say, "Oh, multiculturalism. Political correctness."

Yet he also went on to argue that multicultural education, in principle,
diverted attention from what he believed to be a fundamental purpose
of teaching American history, to provide a basic understanding of the
foundations of American institutions. Thompson explained:

Now, as far as the theory of multiculturalism, I reject it. [If] a person comes
from, say, from China to the United States, on one level, their heritage is
Chinese. But on another level, their heritage does come from England and
from ancient Greece because the institutions of the United States, like democracy, they don't come from China, they come from England and ancient
Greece. Now, my heritage is Irish. We're supposed to hate the British, right?
For what they did to Ireland? But I don't identify. I mean on a cultural level,
I'm proud to be an Irish American and all that stuff. But no, I identify with
England much more because this is where democracy came from. This is, you
know, the English common law. This is where all that kind of good stuff
comes from. It doesn't come from Ireland. They were barbarians there.

By emphasizing distinct cultural heritages, Thompson claimed, the curriculum created inauthentic sources of identity.

Jerry Ciani similarly opposed attempts to revise history. Reacting to
recent controversies over depictions of Christopher Columbus, he
complained,

I see people who want to have things both ways. They want to have their
cake and eat it too, and that's why I find that most of these revisionists, they
want to include this, but including means excluding something else. They're

not all inclusive. It's like everything that's from Europe is no good. Everything from someplace else is fine, you know.

Now, I have my own particular pet peeve. I happen to be Italian Catholic. I belong to the Knights of Columbus. Do you know what it's like for me to look up and see them trying to blame all the evils on Christopher Columbus? The man was a sailor; all he wanted to do was explore. What makes you think he had a say in how Spain was going to treat the colonies after he left? You know, that upsets me. Things like this, you're not giving the full story.

Echoing concerns of critics such as Arthur Schlesinger Jr. in *The Disuniting of America*, other teachers moved beyond pragmatic issues to the social implications of emphasizing diversity. Too much emphasis on ethnic differences, some feared, would lead to social fragmentation among students and undermine a sense of unity their schools were struggling to achieve. Linda Peters explained:

> But what you're trying to do here is you're trying to create community in the school. And . . . if you have a diverse community to begin with, you're making them come together! You're not trying to separate them. You're not trying to keep the Blacks here and the Latinos there. You try to bring them together. Right?

Likewise, Marie Sanchez rejected the idea that schools should promote separate and distinct cultures. By determining friendship patterns and encouraging group identities, the focus on ethnicity, she observed, balkanized social groups.

In addition to these remarks, some teachers offered more sophisticated critiques of oversimplification and essentialism that characterize the construction of multicultural education in secondary education. For example, while Lewis Kramer agreed that students enjoy learning history that is relevant to their own lives, he questioned the therapeutic purposes of multicultural aims and the assumption that cultural identification would enhance students' self-esteem. His observations reminded me of comments from Texas textbook committee members who felt that critics of textbook knowledge lost sight of the teacher's role in the classroom.

> My view is that students have, students develop a better sense of self and self-esteem out of accomplishment, not out of what they read in books. And so the kinds of things that one needs to do in terms of creating politically engaged students, students who have an ability to see things critically are, they're probably more questions of pedagogy—how one teaches and how one engages students, than they are the material. I'm not denying the material is important but I think that those other questions are in some ways prior to [what is

taught], because, I mean, you could teach all this material in ways that would put students to sleep.

James Vargas said that educators, including some of his colleagues, were becoming overly presumptive about the meaning and significance of ethnicity. As a minority teacher, he felt pressured to demonstrate an allegiance to Spanish-speaking students.

> Until last year I taught some bilingual classes; that's because I speak Spanish. I never wanted to, but they didn't have anyone to teach those classes so I filled in. I never wanted to, I told them. So, this colleague of mine says to me, "now, wouldn't you want to help your people?" I said, "what do you mean, my people?" You know, I have more in common with, I know more about Joe DiMaggio. What do you mean, my people? I know more about American history than the history of Latin American countries. What do you mean my people? I don't understand the term "my people."

Similarly, Walters questioned the belief that students need to identify with faculty of their own group in order to succeed in school. As a white teacher in a predominantly nonwhite school, she felt she had no difficulty establishing a rapport with many of her students regardless of their ethnic backgrounds.

> It's important when a child comes to my classroom that they feel that they are valued. But I don't know, on the other hand, I'm torn about this myself to tell you the truth. I don't see why I can't be a role model for some black person or a Chinese person or a Spanish person. And you know, I think I have been. And I think that's a more important lesson.

In sum, while these teachers found global studies to be a reasonable and valuable means of introducing knowledge about cultures throughout the world, they were less convinced of the need to present American history from multicultural perspectives, especially if these perspectives appeared to compromise a basic understanding of common experiences and institutions or reflected what they thought to be flawed assumptions about the relationship between student motivation and curricular content.

## EXPLAINING TEACHERS' PERSPECTIVES ON DIVERSITY

There is a striking paradox between the range of diversity that surrounds teachers in the schools I visited and their tendency to overlook or minimize its relevance in the curriculum. At first glance, teachers' attitudes toward multicultural education may create the impression that they are incognizant of or indifferent to the racial and ethnic diversity that exists in their schools. But this is not the case. Teachers do recognize the diversity of their students and, in some cases, are quite proud of it. Nearly boasting about their students' varied backgrounds, a few assured me that theirs was probably the most diverse school I would find.

> This campus is probably the most multiethnic campus in the entire country. The *New York Times* did an article on that. I would say that the majority of our students, it changes from year to year, but forty percent [are] Hispanic, [there are] a lot of Asian students, a certain percentage of African Americans. I would say that at any class at any time, I could have thirty different countries. I could go around the room and not hit the same country twice.

"My students are as diverse as they come," Ciani said. "I would say that predominantly they're from the islands, the Caribbean—Haiti, St. Lucia, that whole community is very well represented in my school. We're starting to get a tremendous amount of Eastern Europeans, the Russian community."

Missing from these observations, however, is a deeper understanding of how the diversity these teachers enthusiastically describe might create particular student needs and warrant changes in traditional modes of teaching. Instead, most teachers believed their schools were doing enough to address, or at least cope with, issues of diversity. As indicated in the excerpts above, some seemed to think their schools were practicing multicultural education simply by being diverse, while others related how different cultural backgrounds gained recognition through the social life of the school. Matthew Brennan described the multicultural activities of his Brooklyn high school as follows:

> They have a Jewish club, I think there's an Arab club . . . several others. I think there's an African American, there's a Hispanic, sure. And a couple of weeks ago, they had the international cafe. A lot of the groups got together and all the foods were on display. Once in a while they have some ethnic dances down in the cafeteria during lunch. A few weeks ago, there was an Arab dance recital, and I think there was a Greek dance recital. As far as the League of Nations, it would be difficult, probably in New York City, to find a more diverse population than we have. You name it.

The activities in Brennan's account typify the ways in which many schools define and practice multicultural education. Sandra Dickerson wrote:

Whenever anyone asks if there is multicultural education at the Cambridge
Rindge and Latin School, the answer usually includes expounding upon the
rich diversity of the student population. It is true that there are over 130 different cultures represented at CRLS. In some classrooms, if there are 30 students
present, often there may be 27 distinctly different cultures present. The principal celebrates these differences by prominently displaying 30 or 40 flags from
different countries around the world in the cafeteria.[12]

But, as Dickerson expresses so well, "flags and warm brown, black,
and yellow bodies do not a multiculturalism make."[13] These approaches
to multicultural education exemplify what theorists call an additive
model of multicultural education. According to this model, multiculturalism is global studies. Multiculturalism is the rich diversity of student
bodies and the celebration of that diversity through annual multicultural
fairs. Though indicative of an important shift away from cultural homo-
geneity, the mere acknowledgement of diversity does not approximate
the form of multicultural education critical theorists have in mind.
Rather, the emphasis on cultural styles in conventional multicultural
practices belies the significance of social differences, and in particular,
how racial constructs shape group relations and patterns of inequality.
Christine Sleeter described the construction of multicultural lessons in
one school she researched as follows:

Americans of color were lumped with immigrants who were collectively
defined as "other," bringing customs that are, at best, interesting to learn
about and share when there is time. "Whiteness" was taken as the norm, as
natural. When teachers told me about "multicultural lessons" or "multicultural bulletin boards," what they usually drew my attention to was the flat
representations of people of color that had been added; multidimensional representations of whiteness throughout the school were treated as a neutral
background not requiring comment.[14]

One consequence of such messages, Sleeter concludes, is that schools
teach students "that race no longer structures access to resources in the
U.S., and that America's racial groups stand in equal status to one
another, differentiated only by customs in which anyone can participate."[15]

Popular models of multicultural education aim to reverse prejudicial
attitudes among individuals while ignoring conflictual race relations and
structural impediments to opportunity.[16] These models cannot achieve
the goal of critical pedagogy, which, in contrast, seeks to situate group
identities in a relational context[17] and to incorporate students' histories
and experiences as a basis of involvement, empowerment, and critique.[18]

Instead of critically examining and reconstructing what is taught, additive approaches celebrate diversity as mere variety. As William Pinar has put it, they fail "to understand curriculum as a racial text" and to understand America "as fundamentally a racialized place."[19]

## STUDENTS: THE NEW DIVERSITY

The tendency among teachers to overlook group identities and relations may be attributed to two factors—their effort to maintain a color-blind perspective toward both the curriculum and their students, and their perceptions of students' own interests and capabilities. Undoubtedly the racial and ethnic makeup of student populations has changed over the past thirty years, and quite remarkably in recent years. While diversity in the 1960s and 1970s referred to groups broadly categorized as Latino(a) Americans, African Americans, Asian Americans, Native Americans, and European Americans, the diversity in many of today's public high schools encompasses students from a far greater number of countries and cultural backgrounds. Variations within categories—between Puerto Ricans and Salvadorans, Haitians and Dominicans, southeast Indians and Cambodians—complicate neatly defined pan-ethnic classifications and sources of identification. For teachers, diversity has become inordinately complex compared to their own educational and early teaching experiences.

Adding to the mix are student differences based on social class and time of arrival to the United States. Many students are recent immigrants who, at least according to teachers, desire to become integrated into their new schools. Initially, they are likely to befriend peers who share a similar background and to maintain a sense of ethnic identity during their freshman and sophomore years when language barriers separate them from English-speaking students. Walters observed:

> I think if the students were born here, they tend to identify *less* with their ethnic group. Whereas, the Dominican kids that are born in the Dominican Republic come here to this country, and they're very tight in the school. They tend to be in the bilingual programs so they hang around together. But then, I'll meet a kid that's born here, who's not a bilingual, and they don't really come out and let you know they're Dominican until after you get to know them, and you find out they're from the Dominican Republic or their family's from the Dominican Republic. So they tend to let that be known less. I see the Bangladeshi kids, they're very tight, and they tend to be in similar classes. There's a West Indian group, so I think it's the fact that if they've recently

come, they're looking for somebody that can show them around and has the same culture as they do.

However, the meaningfulness of ethnic ties subsides as students grow more comfortable socializing outside of their ethnic groups. They eventually want to be American, teachers say, and being American means leaving distinct cultural characteristics at home. Some students change their given names to popular American names. Their behaviors are more consistent with patterns of assimilation in the first half of the twentieth century than with expressions of multiculturalism in the 1960s or identity-based politics in the 1990s. Their desires and aspirations do not support a view of social actors intent on expressing ethnic pride or participating in movements focused on racial and ethnic identities. Consequently, Peters noted, students at her school in Queens sometimes feel confused by the dual messages they receive in a society that espouses multiculturalism but still requires assimilation. She said:

> And what they came here for was to become part of the system. And to some extent, some of them are going to go all the way, some are going to make it, and go on to colleges, good colleges, and get wonderful educations. And some will just graduate high school and have, you know, just regular jobs. But that's why they came here, and so, on the one hand there's that drive to become quote unquote American, to make it, to speak English, and know who Jackson is, and know who Lincoln is, George Washington. On the other hand, they're hearing, "Oh, you should be proud of your food."

Because teachers perceive students as wanting to gain acceptance and to get ahead, they avoid drawing attention to ethnic distinctions in their classrooms. As Margaret Bronson put it,

> They *want to blend in*. [They say] "Please don't call on me and ask me about what we do to celebrate Ramadan. I don't want to let anybody know who I am. Don't call on me." It's the Americanization of everyone, you know, homogenization. It's happening here at a tremendous rate, a tremendous rate, and I'm sure it's causing some difficulties at home. I hear it from the kids.

The new diversity of the 1990s challenged teachers to simultaneously acknowledge students' differences and to respect their desire to blend in with their classmates. Clearly, teachers recognize the impact of homogenization. But they saw no reason to reverse the process. Instead, they attempted to ignore racial and ethnic differences altogether.

## POLITICAL CONSCIOUSNESS AND
## HISTORICAL KNOWLEDGE

Central to theories of reconstructive change is the notion of students as critical thinkers and social agents who might actively participate in a democratic society if they could see themselves in history and feel empowered by their access to new knowledge. Some teachers agreed that students showed unusual interest in topics such as the women's and Civil Rights movements. Recalling heightened reactions to a unit she teaches on slavery, Sarah Berger explained:

> Certainly for the African American students, it definitely made them sit up more and take more notice. . . . there are no white kids in this school. Everybody sort of saw that [unit on slavery] as their own story. And I try, when I teach slavery, to talk about the universal idea of slavery. I mean we focus on the slavery of Africans by the Europeans, but, we talk about it also as a universal. . . . So they obviously have a desire to learn more about their own personal backgrounds, and they talk about, in their essays about [their] background, family, and heritage, they're really into that.

Describing his effort to introduce material relevant to the heritages of Caribbean students, Ray Johnson gave a similar example:

> It really does mean something to some of the kids. Because when you can demonstrate their part in history, kids perk up. I'll give you an example. . . . I was reading an article on the War of 1812, and during the course of reading the article, I noticed that there were 208 Dominican men of color, and they were at that battle, and there were also Haitians at that battle. So, I mention that. Kids say, "What?" I said, "Yes, at the Battle of 1812, there were 208 Dominican men, and there were active men who were also Haitian." But when kids can see that they were there, that they were involved, and that they had a part in this country's history, it changes everybody's perspective when they can actually see [they are] a part of what went on here in a positive way. That's another thing, because part of what we do is Americanization. No matter what, you know, that's the original reason for social studies is to Americanize the immigrant kids. And that's what we have. I mean that's just a reality here in this school. This is Harlem, but it's no longer the west Harlem of twenty years ago. All right? Now, west Harlem is totally multicultural, and we need to be able to show the students a textbook [in which] they can see some of themselves.

These two teachers' experiences affirm the expectation of critical multicultural theorists that students will feel more enthusiastic about knowledge pertaining to people and events to which they can relate.

However, teachers' portraits of other students in their classes illuminate why they have difficulty cultivating the sense of empowerment and
level of critical consciousness that theorists propose. Several teachers
were dismayed by the fact that students' knowledge of African American figures was limited to Martin Luther King, Rosa Parks, and people
prominent in current media. Kostas, who teaches in Queens, explained
his disappointment:

> They know who Martin Luther King is. They know who Jesse Jackson is.
> They know, of course, who David Dinkins is. They think David Dinkins is
> the greatest mayor in the history of New York City. They don't believe me
> when I tell them he's a gofer. You know what a gofer is, right? Go for coffee?
> And he lost. Why did he lose? If he was a good mayor we would have
> reelected him. Wasn't a good mayor, so we didn't reelect him. . . . Do they
> know who Jesse Owens is? No. Do they know who Jackie Robinson is? Yes.
> Why? Because this year we're celebrating the 50th [anniversary of Robinson's
> breaking the color barrier in baseball]. Do they know who Tiger Woods is?
> Yes. Do they know who Colin Powell is? Yes. So, I mean they know because
> it's in front of their nose. Do they know what the importance of Tiger Woods
> is? *Not* a clue. . . . One day I was talking and I mentioned the Black Panthers.
> *Not* a clue. Not a clue.

For others the primary obstacle to effective teaching was a very low
level of student interest in education, as Kelley explained:

> The people that I know in teaching are in urban education . . . here in New
> York, [and] I know several people who teach in Miami, Chicago, and in Los
> Angeles. And I think we all pretty much have the same experience, that the
> vast majority of students are not that interested in history, see it as a course
> that they *have* to take, *have* to pass, that they don't see as relevant. I think a lot
> of that is probably due to some bad teaching. But I also think that it's due to
> their being teenagers and being wrapped up in their own lives. I think you
> could also point the finger at students coming to high school lacking basic
> skills in reading and writing or not really being able to analyze texts or to think
> critically, to identify bias and assumption within other people's writing. So I
> think that a realistic picture of urban education today really would not include
> a highly motivated student body.

Even when teachers attempt to develop the kinds of critical thinking
and political awareness that theorists advance, they sometimes become
discouraged. Randy MacDonald, who is personally interested in Nica-
raguan history, described his feelings this way:

> I don't want to speak badly of the students but it's very hard for me to say that
> they're interested in very much that's intellectual or academic. . . . So when I

do talk about revolutionary movements in other countries, it really doesn't turn them on. It turns *me* on. I'm interested in it. But even with my passion in these issues, I may catch the attention of some, but I very seldom see a student or hear a student make connections. The poor people in Central America are trying to organize; why aren't the poor people here? You never get that kind of higher level thinking being exercised.

MacDonald remarked on the differences between the political activism of his generation and the apparent apathy among today's youth.

In the sixties, the war was being fought, civil rights, there were so many differ-ent movements and leaders who were constantly in the media. And you couldn't escape. Now they [the students] are more interested in t.v. shows and sports.

I was extremely unusual. I was a draft resister and activist. I was in my senior year in 1970. I didn't organize demonstrations but I was very vocal. . . . So I try to remind myself that I'm the same way now as I was when I was sixteen, but that's extremely unusual. That's exceptionally rare. So just because they're black or brown, or Hispanic, or African-American or they come from work-ing classes or poor families doesn't mean that they're going to be any more receptive.

Bronson recounted her effort to begin a class discussion about move-ments for democracy on the day of our interview.

"Today's the anniversary of Tiananmen Square," I said. "*Eight years* have gone by." "Eight years. I'm shocked, it just seems like yesterday. Aren't you sur-prised?" "No," [students reply.] This is what you get from our youngsters about political events, even current events. You know, I show them a picture of the tanks and the kid. "What a jerk." "Yeah, what a jerk, that's just stupid." . . . "What a jerk," . . . that was their reaction to the picture of the youngster and the tank. "What a jerk." So, it's *hard*. It's very hard. Apathy is our most difficult thing to overcome.

In light of these examples of students' indifference, I asked teachers what, if anything, interests or excites their students. Walters's response was typical. Students, she said, are concerned much more with popular culture—fashion, music, and sports—than with racial, ethnic, or sexual identities. Her students had become so homogenized by consumer goods that she could not distinguish them by class or culture.

Even students of very low socioeconomic background [are] interested in how they dress. I don't know where they get the money, but they're gonna wear good sneakers, and they're gonna wear Ralph Lauren shirts, you know, so it's very hard to tell. And my honest reflection, which I talk about in social studies classes, is maybe the parents of a lot of these students are very different, if you went to their homes and saw their customs. But I think the culture has homogenized these kids, the American culture, the pop culture. They all want the same things. I don't care where they come from, when they're sitting in my class, and when I walk out of the class, I don't see different ethnic groups. There's so much; I don't see that at all. But what I do see is, they're wearing the same jeans, they're wearing the same sneakers or whatever's in vogue. . . . They're listening to the same music . . . they're watching television, and they're seeing the same advertising. They want the same things for themselves.

In contrast to the students Walters describes, Kostas's students puzzled him because they were not even interested in television; none had watched any of the recently aired NBA playoffs. He said, "They *don't* watch t.v. I asked them, 'You watch the Simpsons? What do you watch?' They [said they] chill. They hang out and they chill." Students, he says, are looking for relevance. They want to know why history is relevant to their lives, not as an affirmation of identity as multicultural proponents would posit, but as practical knowledge. For this reason, Kostas devotes more energy to coming up with relevant topics than to using historical insights to raise political consciousness.

> How do you pique the interest of kids who come in here and say, "How's this going to make me money in the future?" They don't realize that the only way you can make money is to learn how to think independently. What teaches you a better way of thinking than to understand what history's all about and seeing how things came to be the way they are? It just makes no sense to me, not to love education, not to love to learn. These kids only learn what they have to learn, only do what they have to do.

Finally, on the few occasions when teachers encourage students to deliberate over social and political issues, it cannot necessarily be assumed, as critical multicultural theorists might predict, that students will take a progressive stance in discussions and debates. Carol Kent, one of two African American teachers in the sample, explained how she has on occasion, raised discussions about race and race relations in her American history course. Yet, some of her students, white and black, had recently signed a petition against her because they felt these discussions divided and caused conflict in the classroom. Like teachers, students seemed to want to adopt a color-blind perspective toward themselves and their peers. Because of the controversy surrounding her teaching approaches, she expressed doubts about whether she could continue teaching classes in American history.

Consistent with Kent's experience, Kelley observed that although her students were quite aware of and disturbed by racial discrimination, they were unlikely to link individual experiences with broader societal issues.

> I think that they do think an awful lot about race and ethnicity, but I think that it's very focused on difference, on simplistic questions of injustice. For example, my students could identify being followed around a department store by a security guard as a racist assumption, but would not be able to tell you why having thirty percent of the ground troops in Vietnam coming from the black community would be racist.

According to several teachers, policies such as affirmative action tended to receive little student support. Galiano recounted how students, embracing an achievement ideology, opposed the school's elimination of a once standard entrance exam.

> It is *unbelievable*. We used to have an exam in this school, an entrance exam. They did away with it due to affirmative action, discriminatory reasons. The school had a vote, because I think we were pushing one of our . . . legislators to support a bill in the state legislature and she did. Ninety percent of the students [wanted] the entrance exam . . . brought back, which is an amazing number considering that we have like a ninety-eight percent minority population in this school. But I think the feeling is, "wait a second, I can do it just as anyone else could."

Describing similar student perspectives at her school, Anne O'Neill explained that students lacked the historical background that would help them to understand affirmative action's purpose.

> They don't think that anybody should be given an advantage. See, and I can understand that, they're fighting for equality, and they want equality, and they don't want to be treated differently because they are black. So why should they be treated differently because they are black, even if it's a positive treatment, because they don't see that. It's a color blind issue, treat us equally. Everybody should be treated the same, and there in the classroom, basically that does happen. You know, just because you're a different race doesn't mean you get a different test. . . . to some degree they see prejudice, I'm not saying they don't see the prejudice, but they just want equity, and they think equity will . . . get them all the answers.

According to the teachers in this sample, for multiple reasons—students' desires to be treated equally, their preoccupations as young adolescents, and their limited interest in social and political issues—they do not expect to generate a high level of critical consciousness in their classrooms or their schools.

Some teachers expressed disappointment with their colleagues as well. Bernstein observed:

> I find a lot of my colleagues don't read. That scares the living daylights out of me. . . . I've got the *Military History Quarterly* here, the *Consumer Reports*, I have the *Smithsonian*, I have my *Newsweek*, I have three or four other publications that I get; I read a book a week. I'm always on top of my subject. And there are four or five people in my department who are basically my age, and we talk books. You can't do that with the new people. They just don't read. They frankly don't know their subject area. I had a teacher come in and ask me, less than a year ago, he came in and said, "Quick, when did the United States enter World War I?" "Don't tell me you're teaching history, [Bernstein replied] "please tell me you're teaching some other subject. Don't tell me you're teaching my subject because you're not teaching it. You don't know it."

Kostas also noted that he had difficulty relating to and respecting other teachers at his school.

> Most of my colleagues say, "You should have been here twenty years ago when there were all Jews and Greeks here. The school was really good then." So, they come to work, and it's like punching a clock. They get in at 8:15, they leave at 2:35. And they can't give a shit about anything in between. Now, I wander around the building in this free period, you know for preparation and things like that, looking for teachers to talk to. Nobody's interested. I mean they're all doing their own lesson plans, and they're marking papers, and they're doing this or doing that. Nobody wants to sit down and talk about what's happening in China, or what's happening in Japan.

### INTERPRETING TEACHERS' PERSPECTIVES

Although research substantiates teachers' claims that high school students lack both a knowledge of and interest in subjects such as American history, teachers' descriptions of student apathy beg the question of why students are so disinterested.[20] Teachers expressed frustration with their clientele, yet most did not look to themselves, to the curriculum, or to the social settings in which they work as possible sources of reform. Instead, they viewed student apathy as being almost irreversible. Neither Galiano nor O'Neill, for example, considered how their own classroom lessons could provide historical background and stimulate a discussion about the notion of color blindness or issues such as affirmative action had they chosen to pursue these topics. If there is a "culture of power" in school classrooms, as some theorists suggest, teachers took little notice of its possibilities. It did not occur to them to consider how students' everyday lives and experiences, or what they are doing when they are "chilling," might be invited into the learning process. Such insights are crucial to appreciating the need for alternative curricula and pedagogies. One wonders how we can expect students to develop a sense of interest, much less passion, for learning when their teachers seem so cynical and powerless.

Teachers' perspectives reveal the positions from which they view curricular ideas and why they may be incapable or perceive themselves as being incapable of carrying out the agendas critical theorists prescribe. However, we must also ask whether their references to inadequate material resources, to state demands, to student apathy, and especially to students' lack of interest in cultural identities, are convenient "outs" that free teachers from the challenge and responsibility of diverging from routine; changing or improving their teaching; engaging students, especially the most apathetic ones; and dealing with controversial subjects such as racial discrimination.

The same can be said for the blindness teachers exhibited toward issues of sexual orientation that were also distinctive about 1990s curricular reforms. Indeed, the very limited response I received to my inquiries about New York City's Rainbow curriculum is telling. While some teachers avoided discussing the Rainbow by claiming that controversies over its agenda applied to primary rather than secondary schooling, others asserted that the subject of sexual orientation should be addressed in the home. As discussed in chapter 4, conflicts over the Rainbow curriculum did stem primarily from disagreements over teaching very young students about diverse families and sexual orientations. But surely topics such as sexual orientation, homophobia, and discrimination against gays and lesbians are relevant to the teaching of history at the secondary level. Nonetheless, the very fact that teachers resisted including sexual identities as part of their notion of multicultural education substantiates the fear among progressive theorists that sexual diversity is receiving even less attention than the delicate topic of race. As I argued in chapter 4, the discomfort with teaching topics related to sexual orientation is due in part to the fact that sexual diversity cannot be integrated as easily into the dominant narrative without transforming that narrative.

Principles of color blindness may help us to understand why teachers deny the significance of racial and cultural differences, but such principles and beliefs in turn raise the question of whether race relations in schools are as color blind as teachers assume and whether color blindness is not, in fact, a problem to be addressed rather than an uncritical and perhaps convenient way to ignore the challenges of addressing diversity in school relations and the curriculum. The teachers I interviewed seemed reluctant to reflect on the ways in which the curriculum, classroom environments, and schools might be made more hospitable to expressing cultural differences. How, for example, might teachers restructure their lessons and the climates of their classrooms so that social differences and traditions such as Ramadan are understood to be topics worth knowing about rather than sources of unease or embarrassment for those who practice them? Yet, few considered the possibility that racial minorities have internalized dominant notions of American identity and are hardly in a position to resist those notions. Instead, teachers were quick to assume that students want to become American and are eager to relinquish their ethnic ties; they read students' behaviors as aspirations to assimilate rather than reflections of a system in which minority interests are excluded or ignored. The fact that students feel uncomfortable about difference was left unexamined as was the dominance of common notions of American identity such as former U.S. presidents Lincoln, Jackson, and Washington; their status in official knowledge was simply assumed.

While several teachers supported the pluralistic "salad bowl" view of American culture now commonly portrayed in history textbooks, they tacitly endorsed traditionally accepted models of the melting pot consistent with their personal experiences and with what they learned in school. Describing the meaning of ethnicity in her family, O'Neill said:

> I think there's a desire in various communities to make that identity strong, to make me consider myself as an Irish American, and you consider yourself an Oriental American. . . . It's not that I walk away from my Irish heritage or that I'm asking my child to do that, or I don't want him to know what his heritage is. I don't want his heritage to be the issue, I guess is what I'm saying. I want him to know it, and I want him to understand, and I want him to appreciate it, but I don't want that to be the issue that runs his life.

Unfortunately, O'Neill misses the fact that her son, who is of European heritage, can choose whether his ethnicity will or will not run his life. Her perspective substantiates the argument that individuals of European heritage think of ethnicity as an option while failing to understand the ways in which race and ethnicity shape the lives of nonwhites regardless of whether or not the latter choose to embrace these sources of identity.[21]

# THE PROMISE OF
# EDUCATIONAL CHANGE

In light of the above critique and of the attitudes and conditions illuminated in teachers' accounts, it is tempting to adopt one of two common views. Yet, I caution against doing so. One is a pessimistic view that teachers have been de-skilled and rendered virtually helpless by the principles of hierarchy, segmentation, and control that govern public schooling. External demands and decision making severely restrict teachers' authority and independence and heighten their sense of alienation. Hence, there is no hope for curricular reforms. This view must be qualified by the fact that some teachers in this sample and in other studies do recognize their potential to reconstruct knowledge and noted a variety of methods they use to teach effectively. For example, Thompson described what he called his subversive method of teaching:

> Unfortunately, the way I usually do it, in fact a lot of teachers do it, is rather than trying to open up this narrative and teach multiple narratives in history . . . we teach the master narrative, and smash it. . . . I don't know how to put it, it's like my class is a class in subversive history almost. I'll say, "let me tell you the master story. And then let me tell you why it's a lot of malarkey."

His students, he believes, appreciate his approach because

> the only teachers they've ever had is [*sic*] teachers who wrapped themselves in the American flag, and taught a more sophisticated version of George Washington chopping down the cherry tree. And to have a guy who's talking about how the United States did all sorts of horrible things, I've sensed that they feel privileged that you know, this is something, they're being told the truth for the first time.

Several teachers showed me examples of journals their students had composed and creative student projects they had supervised. Kramer noted that he incorporated works by Henry Louis Gates, Maya Angelou, and Cornel West as alternatives to the standard curriculum. At the beginning of a semester, Kramer asks his students to investigate the history of their surnames as a lesson about identity. He explained the positive impact of his teaching method on students.

> You know, after thirteen years you've had almost every kind of student. To the extent to which students come to appreciate that you do know, that you're not just presenting uninformed kinds of ideas, they will engage you. There is conversation. Students are interested in discussing. And I think it's kind of

amazing that teenagers would have a discussion about race and sex, or any of those [topics], much less a bunch of black and Hispanic teenagers having it with a middle-aged white man.

By doing their own thing, teachers like Kramer sometimes manage to motivate their students. Their behaviors support the assumptions of institutional theories that predict that although organizations act upon individuals and shape what they do, individuals respond to social structures in ways that defy, elaborate upon, or circumvent convention. Roger Freidland and Robert Alford write:

> Institutions constrain not only the ends to which their behavior should be directed, but the means by which those ends are achieved. They provide individuals with vocabularies of motives and with a sense of self. They generate not only that which is valued, but the rules by which it is calibrated and distributed. Institutions set the limits on the very nature of rationality and, by implication, of individuality. Nonetheless, individuals, groups, and organizations try to use institutional orders to their own advantage.[22]

Students in Kramer's government classes won an annual competition called "We the People" that tests knowledge of the Constitution. Other teachers were sufficiently motivated to participate in special programs such as the American History Culture Project in New York City. Two teachers described taking their classes on field trips to Washington, D.C., each year while another had applied for a scholarship to study the Civil War. To be sure, their sense of empowerment was the exception rather than the rule; nonetheless, they had found ways to make history interesting sometimes as a means of asserting their independence and expressing their own creativity, and other times as a reaction to the limitations of the standard curriculum. At the very least, teachers' innovations and complaints indicate a capacity for resistance. If they were complacent, passive automatons, they would have had very little to say.

An alternative view fails to consider the conditions under which teachers work, the challenges they face in their classrooms, and the ways in which they are treated. Even if teachers agreed with critical versions of multicultural curricular policy, their capacity to implement these policies would still be undermined by their positions in educational bureaucracies and the day-to-day realities of teaching large groups of students for whom history holds little interest and meaning. Were they to embrace new curricular ideas, most teachers would still be hard pressed to fit in more information, more objectives, and more skills, and to find sufficient resources and instructional support to use them. When teachers struggle to cover the topics that appear on regents exams, when they fight to find teaching materials and classroom space, and when they stand before students with limited attention and highly varied abilities, new curricular matters, whether they pertain to diversity or something else, are too abstract and divorced from experience to impel teachers to assume roles as agents of progressive change. In part the problem stems from their limited understanding of diversity and their efforts to be color blind, but it is also related to the obstacles they must overcome just to get through the course of a day, their sense of disempowerment, and the absence of guidance to deal with the degree of diversity they encounter.

As Lisa Delpit contends, reconceptualizing what is to be taught requires a dialogue with those who teach, both to learn the practicalities of teaching new ideas and to better understand how teachers themselves think about issues of diversity and difference.[23] I would add that in order for this dialogue to take place, teachers will first need some assurance and evidence that their views matter and that reforms will address issues that are, as one teacher in the sample put it, "prior to" the curriculum. Critical multicultural theorists contend that teachers must implement a "language of critical pedagogy" that provides students with the skills to

> locate themselves in history, in their own voices, and provide the convictions and compassion necessary for exercising civic courage, taking risks, and furthering the habits, customs, and social relations that are essential to democratic public forms.[24]

Yet, teachers too, need access to democratic public forms and opportunities and motivation to exercise their civic courage. Otherwise, their well-founded sense that no one is listening to them leads to feelings of frustration, futility, and marginalization, which in turn, contribute to cynicism, hopelessness, irritation, and disengagement. The curriculum becomes a nonissue.

Suppose reformers do acknowledge the social conditions and organizational limitations of teachers' work. How do they then begin to address teachers' attitudes toward multicultural education, their perceptions of students' needs, and their efforts to be color blind? Undeniably, these issues are critical obstacles to multicultural curricular change. But again, there have been few discussions about how to initiate reform agendas as part of a dialogue with teachers. On the contrary, reformers commonly identify teachers' inadequacies as the main problem, and propose antiracism workshops as the solution.

We tend to talk *about* teachers and to tell them "here is one more area in which you're lacking." Yet, following theories of critical pedagogy, we know this practice elicits little more than the irritation and defensiveness that emerge in the interviews. Instead, we need to talk *with* teachers, and to persuade them, like students, that their problems are worthy of attention, that their perspectives are real, and that their willingness to try new pedagogical strategies and alternative ways of thinking will be welcomed and rewarded.

While acknowledging my own critique of teachers' attitudes and behaviors, I suggest we refrain from focusing exclusively on their color blindness and their failure to understand the significance of race and ethnicity. Proponents of reconstructive curricular change rightfully encourage teachers to learn new discourses[25] and to move toward examining their own beliefs and prejudices.[26] But with as many mandates as teachers receive and with as little affirmation as they gain, the last thing teachers need to hear is that they don't really know their students, and that they must work on changing their attitudes, on reevaluating their own histories, and on eradicating their stereotypical beliefs. Although this form of introspection is important and necessary, how these issues are presented to teachers is critical to attaining their active participation in curricular reform.

Rather than instructing white teachers to attend workshops in order to become enlightened and aware of their social status and their ignorance and biases, the first step is to listen to their concerns, to accept that some students *are* difficult to teach, and more substantively, to provide practical guidance on how to address multiple identities and backgrounds. When teachers say their students want to blend in, we should ask them to think about the reasons for students' preferences—past and current discrimination and exclusion, dominant cultural norms, their need for social acceptance, and so on—but at the same time, we should avoid dismissing or contradicting what teachers observe and hear, and expecting them to have figured out how to treat diversity when it remains a complex problem among theorists.

In assessing the possibilities of enacting a critical pedagogy, Giroux and Roger Simon, for example, raise some important questions teachers are likely to ask themselves when introducing new lessons:

> What constitutes useful knowledge? Is it the same for all students no matter what their gender, class, race, ethnicity, age, or geographic region? If not, then how can I cope intellectually, emotionally, and practically with such diversity and social difference? What if the teachers' view of useful knowledge differs from what students and their families think? . . . How far can we go in doing critical pedagogy if people are not interested in our agenda or see it as suppressing theirs?[27]

I quote these questions merely to suggest that if critical theorists, who are not teaching indifferent sixteen-year-olds in crowded classrooms five days a week, have yet to find answers to these questions, why do we expect teachers to already have them?

What can be gained from listening to teachers' accounts is not another opportunity to say, "aha, more cynical white teachers who don't understand race," but rather a means of learning why teachers feel and think the way they do. If a dialogue is to take place, and if we are to advance by having it, we must reflect on what they are telling us even if, and especially if, their words are inconsistent with what critical theorists want to hear. Policy makers, activists, and multicultural theorists struggle over how history should be taught and whose knowledge should count. Although these debates are critical to moving the curriculum in new directions, they must involve teachers without whom there will be no reforms.

## NOTES

1. The data in this chapter are based on semistructured in-depth interviews with thirty randomly selected high school social studies teachers in New York City public schools. The interviews were conducted by phone or in school classrooms, libraries, private homes, department lounges, and local diners. They ranged in length from one-half hour to more than two hours. The teachers interviewed were among those who agreed to participate in the study. Their names have been changed to ensure confidentiality. Although I use the term "teachers" in this chapter and throughout the book, I am not suggesting that the responses of these teachers are generalizable to all teachers.

2. New York State Social Studies Review and Development Committee, *One Nation, Many Peoples: A Declaration of Cultural Interdependence* (Albany: New York State Education Department, 1991), 25.

3. New York State, *One Nation, Many Peoples*, 13.

4. Stanley Aronowitz and Henry A. Giroux, *Education Still Under Siege*, 2d ed. (Westport, Conn.: Bergin & Garvey, 1993).

5. Aronowitz and Giroux, *Education*, 40.

6. Aronowitz and Giroux, *Education*, 46.

7. Pierre Bourdieu, *The Field of Cultural Production* (New York: Columbia University Press, 1993), 10.

8. Bourdieu, *Cultural Production*, 14.

9. W. Richard Scott, "Unpacking Institutional Arguments," in *The New Institutionalism in Organizational Analysis*, ed. Paul DiMaggio and Walter Powell (Chicago: University of Chicago Press, 1991), 164–82.

10. Aronowitz and Giroux, *Education*, 37.

11. Aronowitz and Giroux, *Education*, 37.

12. Sandra Dickerson, "The Blind Men (Women) and the Elephant: A Case for

a Comprehensive Multicultural Education Program at the Cambridge Rindge and Latin School," in *Freedom's Plow*, ed. Theresa Perry and James W. Fraser (New York: Routledge, 1993), 71.

13. Dickerson, "Blind Men," 71.

14. Christine E. Sleeter, "How White Teachers Construct Race," in *Race, Identity, and Representation in Education*, ed. Cameron McCarthy and Warren Crichlow (New York: Routledge, 1993), 166–67.

15. Sleeter, "White Teachers," 166.

16. Cameron McCarthy, "After the Canon: Knowledge and Ideological Representation in the Multicultural Discourse on Curriculum Reform," in *Race, Identity, and Representation in Education*, ed. Cameron McCarthy and Warren Crichlow (New York: Routledge, 1993), 289–305.

17. Henry A. Giroux, "Modernism, Postmodernism, and Feminism: Rethinking the Boundaries of Educational Discourse," in *Postmodernism, Feminism, and Cultural Politics*, ed. Henry A. Giroux (Albany, N.Y.: SUNY Press, 1991), 48–49.

18. Henry A. Giroux and Peter McLaren, *Critical Pedagogy, the State and Cultural Struggle,* ed. Henry A. Giroux and Peter McLaren (Albany, N.Y.: SUNY Press, 1989), 125–51.

19. William F. Pinar, "Notes on Understanding Curriculum As a Racial Text," in *Race, Identity, and Representation in Education,* ed. Cameron McCarthy and Warren Crichlow (New York: Routledge, 1993), 62.

20. See James W. Loewen, *Lies My Teacher Told Me* (New York: New Press, 1995); and Robert Lerner, Althea K. Nagai, and Stanley Rothman, *Molding the Good Citizen* (Westport, Conn.: Praeger, 1995).

21. See Sleeter, "White Teachers," 165. Also, see Richard Alba, *Ethnic Identity: The Transformation of White America* (New Haven, Conn.: Yale University Press, 1990), and Mary Waters, *Ethnic Options* (Berkeley: University of California Press, 1990).

22. Roger Friedland and Robert R. Alford, "Bringing Society Back In: Symbols, Practices, and Institutional Contradictions," in *The New Institutionalism in Organizational Analysis*, ed. Paul DiMaggio and Walter W. Powell (Chicago: University of Chicago Press, 1991), 251.

23. Lisa Delpit, *Other People's Children* (New York: New Press, 1995).

24. Giroux, "Modernism, Postmodernism, and Feminism," 47.

25. Delpit, *Other People's Children*, 152–166.

26. Delpit, *Other People's Children*, 179.

27. Henry Giroux and Roger Simon, "Popular Culture and Critical Pedagogy," in *Critical Pedagogy, the State, and Cultural Struggle,* ed. Henry Giroux and Peter McLaren (Albany, N.Y.: SUNY Press, 1989), 250–51.

# 6

# Whose Knowledge Counts?
# Expanding the Debate

How should schools present different groups in history? To what extent should they recognize and encourage distinct identities? These questions will continue to fuel battles over school knowledge as American society experiences accelerating demographic change. While minority groups continue to pressure for representation, tolerance, and recognition, those who wish to preserve a corpus of knowledge that legitimizes their own values, experiences, and beliefs are likely to resist efforts to make official knowledge more inclusive. Debates between parents, interest groups, and scholars in sites such as Texas and New York illustrate the intensity of these struggles and the extent to which school knowledge has become a prime arena in the culture wars.

However, the central theme of this book is that the cultural politics of educational reform are not the main impediment to realizing curricular transformations. Instead, what counts as official knowledge is shaped by decisions made independently of the kinds of ideologies and concerns that inform cultural struggles. When social actors conceptualize the problem of selecting knowledge, they do so from very different positions, assumptions, and expectations. Parents and interest groups attempt to pressure state and local officials who make curricular policies; scholars present their ideas in academic forums and publications quite apart from the settings in which decisions about secondary education occur. Yet, despite these variations, parents, interest groups, and critical theorists share a conception of school knowledge as a cultural repository of moral codes, a means of pursuing social justice, or a basis of intellectual inquiry, depending on their positions. They treat school knowledge as a body of ideas and meanings and evaluate knowledge in terms of its capacity to instill values and preserve tradition, to inspire political consciousness and activism, to build self-esteem, or to develop critical thinking skills, again depending on the perspectives of each group.

In contrast, those who make the real decisions about "official" knowledge approach choices about knowledge and behave in ways that attempt to deny an explicit politics of values. Operating according to both cognitive and structural frameworks that minimize controversy, decision makers avoid overt political decisions and relegate debate about ideas to a realm they perceive to be beyond their jurisdictions. Discourse about ideas, according to educators and publishers, as well as state and local administrators, occurs only among those who read too much into the textbooks, misinterpret the "facts," or are trying to use the school curriculum to further their particular social agendas. As a result, the framing of knowledge as facts devoid of cultural, moral, and ideological meanings distances these agendas from professional decision making. Contrary to the aim of critical theorists to make the social construction of knowledge visible, the fundamental relationship between knowledge and social interests is denied.

Whether we examine school textbooks, curricular policies, or other sources of "official" knowledge, we cannot understand their content apart from the institutional rubrics and organizational systems in which they are produced. Decision makers' behaviors and perspectives are a function not only of how they understand their occupational roles and interests, but also their location in contexts bound by particular priorities and constraints. At the state level, decisions are driven by the need to mediate conflict and fulfill expectations of educational organization; at the level of institutional practice, they are structured by bureaucratic procedures; at the professional level, decisions are governed by a logic of technocratic rationality; at the commercial level, they are motivated by what sells.

Examining the institutional processes and outcomes of educational decision making leaves us with a rather dissatisfying picture; the selection of knowledge seems to have little to do with questions of meaning—what should children be taught, whose knowledge counts? It appears that reproduction theorists are basically right. Even when concepts such as inclusion and multicultural education become a part of the official curriculum as they certainly seemed to over the past three decades, paradigmatic shifts in knowledge at the level of secondary education do not occur. A liberal, pluralist framework remains intact despite an increase in the variety of group identities represented.

But while the obstacles to transformative change support a reproductive account, reproduction does not occur by excluding new knowledges altogether. Nor are dominant groups necessarily or actively engaged in efforts to maintain their worldviews. No such actions are required. Reproduction occurs because critical reflection, the aim that radical progressive reformers pursue and value, is largely absent from decision-making processes that are mired in a technocratic logic. Bureaucratic procedures, curricular policy formation, textbook production, are processes devoid of serious questions about what is to be taught or discourse about how knowledge might be different. Ideas such as diversity, so controversial and provocative in the public and academic realm, become diluted in these sites of implementation and decision making.

As a result, radical shifts in official knowledge are unlikely because decisions about knowledge production and selection are not about transforming the curriculum; they are about management—managing political conflict, managing mass education, managing classrooms, managing profits and losses. The implications of these management strategies for teaching students about diversity are clear. At each point of educational decision making, these factors soften the edges and potency of new ideas. Concepts such as diversity lose their potential impact as state and local officials strive for balance among competing views and promulgate middle-of-the-road policies, publishers cope with market demands by adding photographs of minority families in their texts, textbook committees search for photos of minority families in the texts and check them off their lists, and teachers dismiss multicultural education as a trendy buzzword or define it simplistically as a culture fair. While official knowledge may change, it does not change in ways that dramatically alter our notions of American identity.

My concern is not with who is right or wrong in the culture wars; it is with the problem of ignoring these obstacles to critically evaluating what is taught. Because the concept of diversity has become so common and so familiar, we are easily lulled into thinking that significant educational transformation is occurring. Yet, at a time when schools are becoming more diverse, when they most need to come to terms with cultural and social differences, the knowledge they have at their disposal is packaged in ways that fail to stimulate not only the kinds of goals critical theorists advance—historical consciousness, liberation and empowerment, critical pedagogy—but also a basic interest in history, culture, and social relations. Because new knowledges and debates about new knowledges are resisted, trivialized, or overshadowed by instructional imperatives, schools lack a language and a logic with which to help both students and teachers understand the meaning and significance of the multiple racial, ethnic, and sexual identities that now occupy the hallways and classrooms of their schools. As such, they are left ill equipped to appreciate and learn from the diversity they encounter except in superficial ways.

If the gap between ideas, policies, and implementation is so wide, what is the possibility of realizing curricular transformations that reconstruct our notions of identity? By emphasizing the extent to which institutional contexts and practices impede meaningful change, I do not want to suggest that they are an insurmountable barrier. To do so would be to forget our own participation in learning, conceptualizing, and teaching. Reconstructing school knowledge may require making a stronger connection between theories of multicultural education and critical pedagogy in academic scholarship and the experiences of teachers and students in everyday school life. While much of what I have discussed pertains to differences between matters at stake in cultural politics and issues germane to educational decision making, there is an equally large divide between the ideals envisioned in theories of curricular change and the preoccupations of those involved in providing and receiving education in public schools. I was struck by the comments of Texas textbook committee members who contrasted books that scholars would want to read with books that would work in the classroom, as well as by New York City teachers whose ideas about multicultural education and pedagogy seemed so removed from what is now a vast academic literature on racial, ethnic, and sexual identities. Their reactions made an impression not because I thought either group was wrong, but because the curricular visions popular in the literature seemed so out of touch.

Given the dominance of an ethnicity paradigm in current curricular formulations and teachers' perspectives, it seems that the production, selection, and transmission of school knowledge would surely benefit from access to critical theories of racial and cultural identities. Perhaps scholars would do well to disseminate some of the critical ideas that are bound in books and journals on university library shelves to those who might benefit from using them. However, as I argued in chapter 5, if educational and sociological theories are to be relevant in practice, there must be greater dialogue between those who theorize in institutions of higher learning and those who teach in primary and secondary schools. As theorists, we must learn more about how racial, ethnic, and sexual identities are constructed in schools, and how identities are actually being negotiated in these sites of interaction.

Although the literature on multicultural education has grown considerably, there have been few sociological investigations of the contexts in which identities are defined and expressed. How are teachers and students influenced by diversity in everyday school life? How do they make sense of racial and ethnic constructions that are clearly complicated by individual differences in social class, immigrant status, and culture? To what extent are students able to express their sexual identities as part of the multicultural mix? Clearly students bring a great deal with them to the classroom, some of which has little to do with diversity. And even when diversity is an issue, its meaning is unlikely to be as fixed or stagnant as curricular policy sometimes implies. How might students' attitudes toward education and their understanding of race, ethnicity, and sexual orientation inform and perhaps challenge dominant theoretical approaches to reconstructing knowledge and representing diverse experiences?

We can learn much about the promise of new ideas, again, not by espousing or dictating theoretical visions to practitioners, but by critically examining what diversity and different racial, ethnic and cultural identities mean to teachers and students, integrating their experiences and perspectives into our expectations of what might be taught, and critically examining the institutional processes that shape what schools actually teach. Without this information, we risk limiting debates about diversity in education to an oversimplified discussion of pluralism and unity or abandoning school knowledge as a source of meaningful change simply because curricular reforms cannot remedy social and economic inequalities. Either way, we cease to learn how students, teachers, and institutions might benefit from diverse knowledges and transformative ideas, when, in fact, there is still much to know and do.

# Bibliography

Alba, Richard. *Ethnic Identity: The Transformation of White America*. New Haven, Conn.: Yale University Press, 1990.

Altbach, Philip G., Gail P. Kelly, Hugh G. Petrie, and Lois Weis, eds. *Textbooks in American Society*. Albany, N.Y.: SUNY Press, 1991.

Alyson, Sasha. "Fear of the Rainbow." *New York Times*, 30 December 1992, A15.

Anyon, Jean. "Ideology and U.S. History Textbooks." *Harvard Educational Review* 49 (August 1979): 361–86.

Appiah, K. Anthony. "Identity, Authenticity, Survival: Multicultural Societies and Social Reproduction." In *Multiculturalism*, ed. Charles Taylor and Amy Gutmann, 149–63. Princeton, N.J.: Princeton University Press, 1994.

Apple, Michael W. *Ideology and Curriculum*. London: Routledge & Kegan Paul, 1979.

———. *Education and Power*. Boston: Routledge & Kegan Paul, 1982.

———. "Curricular Form and the Logic of Technical Control." In *Ideology and Practice in Schooling*, ed. Michael W. Apple and Lois Weis, 143–65. Philadelphia: Temple University Press, 1983.

———. "The Culture and Commerce of the Textbook." *Journal of Curriculum Studies* 17 (1985): 147–62.

———. *Official Knowledge*. New York: Routledge, 1993.

Aronowitz, Stanley, and Henry A. Giroux. *Education Still Under Siege*, 2d ed. Westport, Conn.: Bergin & Garvey, 1993.

Banks, James A. *Educating Citizens in a Multicultural Society*. New York: Teachers' College Press, 1997.

Barbanel, Josh. "Fernandez Modifies Parts of Curriculum about Gay Parents." *New York Times*, 27 January 1993, A1, B3.

———. "Under 'Rainbow,' a War: When Politics, Morals, and Learning Mix." *New York Times*, 27 December 1992, I34.

Barna, Joel. "The Texas Textbook Controversy." House Study Group Special Legislative Report. *Texas State Archives* 101 (May 1984).

Belluck Pam, "Conservative School Board Gains Turned Out to Be No Revolution." *New York Times*, 29 April 1996, B2.

Berger, Joseph. "A Mix of Earlier Skirmishes Converges in the Rainbow Curriculum Battle." *New York Times*, 3 December 1992, B4.

————. "New Diversity Old Hat in Some Schools." *New York Times,* 22 June 1991, I25, 26.

————. "Teaching about Gay Life Is Pressed by Chancellor." *New York Times,* 17 November 1992, B3.

Bernstein, Basil. *Class, Codes, and Control.* New York: Schocken, 1975.

Bernstein, Harriet. "The New Politics of Textbook Adoption." *Phi Delta Kappan* (March 1985): 463–66.

Bloom, Alan. *The Closing of the American Mind.* New York: Simon & Schuster, 1987.

Booth, William. "Diversity and Division." *Washington Post Weekly,* 2 March 1998, vol. 15, 6–7, national edition.

Bourdieu, Pierre, and Jean-Claude Passeron. *Reproduction in Education, Society, and Culture.* London: Sage, 1977.

Bourdieu, Pierre. *The Field of Cultural Production.* New York: Columbia University Press, 1993.

California State Board of Education, "History-Social Science Framework for California Public Schools Kindergarten through Grade Twelve." Sacramento, Calif.: California State Department of Education, 1998.

Carnoy, Martin. "Education, State, and Culture in American Society." In *Critical Pedagogy, the State, and Cultural Struggle,* ed. Henry A. Giroux and Peter McLaren, 3–23. Albany, N.Y.: SUNY Press, 1989.

Carnoy, Martin and Henry M. Levin. *Schooling and Work in the Democratic State.* Stanford, Calif.: Stanford University Press, 1985.

Chambliss, Daniel. "Nursing Ethics." Ph.D. diss., Yale University, 1982.

Cohen, Michael D., and James G. March. *Leadership and Ambiguity.* New York: McGraw-Hill, 1974.

Cohen, Muriel. "Critics Say Textbooks Dull, Call for Higher Standards." *Boston Sunday Globe,* 1 December 1985.

Cornbleth, Catherine, and Dexter Waugh. *The Great Speckled Bird.* New York: St. Martin's, 1995.

Coser, Lewis A., Charles Kadushin, and Walter W. Powell. *Books: The Culture and Commerce of Publishing.* New York: Basic, 1982.

Currey, Virginia. "The Politics of Textbook Adoption." *PS* 21, no.1 (Winter 1988).

Dale, Roger. "Education and the Capitalist State." In *Cultural and Economic Reproduction in Education: Essays on Class, Ideology, and the State,* ed. Michael W. Apple. London, Routledge & Kegan Paul, 1982.

Davis, Rod. "Deep in the Heart of Textbooks." *Boston Globe Magazine,* 30 October 1983.

DelFattore, Joan. *What Johnny Shouldn't Read: Textbook Censorship in America.* New Haven, Conn.: Yale University Press, 1992.

Delpit, Lisa. *Other People's Children.* New York: New Press, 1995.

DeSilva, Bruce. "Schoolbooks: A Question of Quality." *Hartford Courant,* 15–18 June 1986, special report: 1–20.

Dickerson, Sandra. "The Blind Men (Women) and the Elephant: A Case for a Comprehensive Multicultural Education Program at the Cambridge Rindge and Latin School." In *Freedom's Plow,* ed. Theresa Perry and James W. Fraser, 65–89. New York: Routledge, 1993.

Dillon, Sam. "Understanding America's Diversity." *New York Times*, 16 February 1990, A34.

———. "The School Board's Confusing Signals." *New York Times*, 12 December 1992, I22.

———. "Curriculum Issues Fuel Races for School Boards." *New York Times*, 24 March 1993, B1.

———. "Voters Show Increased Interest in School Elections." *New York Times*, 4 May 1993, B8.

———. "After Moral Debate, Voters Shape Schools' Future." *New York Times*, 5 May 1993, B4.

Douglas, Mary. *How Institutions Think*. New York: Syracuse University Press, 1996.

Elson, Ruth. *Guardians of Tradition: American Schoolbooks of the Nineteenth Century*. Lincoln: University of Nebraska Press, 1964.

English, Raymond. "The Politics of Textbook Adoption." *Phi Delta Kappan* (December 1980): 275–78.

Farr, Roger, and Michael A. Tulley. "Do Adoption Committees Perpetuate Mediocre Textbooks?" *Phi Delta Kappan* (March 1985): 467–71.

New York City Board of Education. *Children of the Rainbow*. New York: Board of Education of the City of New York, 1990.

Fiske, Edward B. "Lessons." *New York Times*, 7 February 1990, B5.

FitzGerald, Frances. *America Revised*. New York: Vintage, 1980.

Follett, Robert. "The School Textbook Adoption Process." *Book Research Quarterly* 1, no. 2 (Summer 1985): 19–23.

Frank, David John, Evan Schofer, and John Charles Torres. "Rethinking History: Change in the University Curriculum: 1910–90." *Sociology of Education* (October 1994): 231–42.

Friedland, Roger, and Robert R. Alford. "Bringing Society Back In: Symbols, Practices, and Institutional Contradictions." In *The New Institutionalism in Organizational Analysis*, ed. Paul DiMaggio and Walter W. Powell, 232–63. Chicago: University of Chicago Press, 1991.

Gabler, Mel, and Norma Gabler. *What Are They Teaching Our Children?* Wheaton, Ill.: Victor Books, 1987.

Gagnon, Paul, and the Bradley Commission on History in the Schools, ed. *Historical Literacy*. Boston: Houghton Mifflin, 1989.

Giroux, Henry A. "Schooling as a Form of Cultural Politics: Toward a Pedagogy of and for Difference." In *Critical Pedagogy, the State, and Cultural Struggle*, ed. Henry Giroux and Peter McLaren, 125–51. New York: SUNY Press, 1989.

———. *Ideology, Culture and the Process of Schooling*. Philadelphia: Temple University Press, 1981.

———. "Modernism, Postmodernism, and Feminism: Rethinking the Boundaries of Educational Discourse." In *Postmodernism, Feminism, and Cultural Politics*, ed. Henry A. Giroux, 1–59. Albany, N.Y.: SUNY Press, 1991.

Giroux, Henry A., and Roger Simon, "Popular Culture and Critical Pedagogy." In *Critical Pedagogy, the State, and Cultural Struggle*, ed. Henry A. Giroux and Peter McLaren, 236–52. Albany, N.Y.: SUNY Press, 1989.

Giroux, Henry A., and Peter McLaren, eds. *Critical Pedagogy, the State, and Cultural Struggle*. Albany, N.Y.: SUNY Press, 1989.

Gitlin, Todd. *Inside Prime Time*. New York: Pantheon, 1983.

———. *The Twilight of Common Dreams: Why America Is Wracked by Culture Wars*. New York: Henry Holt, 1995.

Glazer, Nathan. *We Are All Multiculturalists Now*. Cambridge, Mass.: Harvard University Press, 1997.

Gouldner, Alvin. *The Dialectic of Ideology and Technology*. New York: Oxford University Press, 1982.

Guillory, John. *Cultural Capital*. Chicago: University of Chicago Press, 1993.

Gusfield, Joseph. *Symbolic Crusade*. Urbana: University of Illinois Press, 1963.

Gutmann, Stephanie. "The Curriculum That Ate New York." *Insight on the News* 9 (15 March 1993): 7–11.

Henneberger, Melinda. "Supporters of AIDS Pledge Criticize Other Programs." *New York Times*, 6 September 1992, I51.

Hirsch, E. D. Jr. *Cultural Literacy*. Boston: Houghton Mifflin, 1987.

Hiss, Tony. "The End of the Rainbow." *New Yorker*, 12 April 1993: 43–54.

Hunter, James Davison. *Culture Wars*. New York: Basic, 1991.

Jackson, Kenneth T., and Barbara B. Jackson, "Why the Time is Right to Reform the History Curriculum. In *Historical Literacy*, ed. Paul Gagnon and the Bradley Commission on History in the Schools, 3–15. Boston: Houghton Mifflin, 1989.

Keith, Sherry. "Choosing Textbooks: A Study of Instructional Materials Selection Processes for Public Education." *Book Research Quarterly* 1, no. 2 (Summer 1985): 24–37.

Killian, Michael. "Local Control—Vanishing Myth in Texas." *Phi Delta Kappan* (November 1984): 192–95.

Kliebard, Herbert M. *The Struggle for the American Curriculum 1893–1958*. 2d ed. New York: Routledge & Kegan Paul, 1986.

Kozol, Jonathan. *Savage Inequalities*. New York: Crown, 1991.

Lerner, Robert, Althea K. Nagai, and Stanley Rothman. *Molding the Good Citizen*. Westport, Conn.: Praeger, 1995.

Liston, Daniel. "Have We Explained the Relationship between Curriculum and Capitalism? An Analysis of the Selective Tradition." *Educational Theory* 34, no.2 (Summer 1984): 241–53.

Loewen, James W. *Lies My Teacher Told Me*. New York: New Press, 1995.

Marks, Peter. "Fernandez Silently Sits in Real-Life People's Court." *New York Times*, 11 February 1993, B2.

Marshall, J. Dan. "With a Little Help from Some Friends: Publishers, Protesters, and Texas Textbook Decisions." In *The Politics of the Textbook*, ed. Michael W. Apple and Linda K. Christian-Smith, 56–77. New York: Routledge, 1991.

———. 1991. "State-Level Textbook Selection Reform: Toward the Recognition of Fundamental Control." In *Textbooks in American Society*, ed. Philip G. Altbach, Gail P. Kelly, Hugh G. Petrie, and Lois Weis, 117–43. Albany, N.Y.: SUNY Press, 1991.

McCarthy, Cameron. "After the Canon: Knowledge and Ideological Representation in the Multicultural Discourse on Curriculum Reform." In *Race, Identity, and Representation in Education*, ed. Cameron McCarthy and Warren Crichlow, 289–305. New York: Routledge, 1993.

McLaren, Peter. "White Terror and Oppositional Agency: Towards a Critical Multiculturalism." In *Multicultural Education, Critical Pedagogy, and the Politics of Difference,* ed. Christine E. Sleeter and Peter L. McLaren, 33–70. New York: SUNY Press, 1995.

McNeil, Linda M. *Contradictions of Control.* New York: Routledge & Kegan Paul, 1986.

Meyer, John W. "Organizations as Ideological Systems." In *Leadership and Organizational Culture,* ed. Thomas Sergiovanni and John E. Corbally, 186–205. Urbana: University of Illinois Press, 1984.

Meyer, John W., and Brian Rowan. "Institutionalized Organizations: Formal Structure As Myth and Ceremony." *American Journal of Sociology* 83 (1977): 340–63.

———. "The Structure of Educational Organizations." In *Environments and Organizations,* Marshall W. Meyer and Associates. San Francisco: Jossey-Bass, 1978.

Meyer, John W., and W. Richard Scott. *Organizational Environments: Ritual and Rationality.* Beverly Hills: Sage, 1983.

Moyer, Wayne A. "How Texas Rewrote Your Textbooks." *Science Teacher* (January 1985): 23–27.

Mukerji, Chandra, and Michael Schudson, eds. *Rethinking Popular Culture.* Berkeley: University of California Press, 1991.

Myers, Steven Lee. "Queens School Board Suspended in Fight on Gay-Life Curriculum." *New York Times,* 2 December 1992, A1.

———. "School Board in Queens Shuns Fernandez Meeting." *New York Times,* 3 December 1992, B3.

———. "Few Using Curriculum in Dispute," *New York Times,* 6 December 1992, I53.

———. "Values in Conflict." *New York Times,* 6 October 1992, B1, 6.

Nasaw, David. *Schooled to Order.* New York: Oxford University Press, 1979.

Nash, Gary B., Charlotte Crabtree, and Ross E. Dunn. *History on Trial: Culture Wars and the Teaching of the Past.* New York: Knopf, 1997.

Nelkin, Dorothy. *Science Textbook Controversies and the Politics of Equal Time.* Cambridge, Mass.: MIT Press, 1977.

New York Social Studies Review and Development Committee, *One Nation, Many Peoples: A Declaration of Cultural Interdependence.* Albany: New York State Education Department, 1991.

O'Leary, Catherine. "Education Reform as Cultural Critique: The Knowledge/ Power Boundary of Liberal Political Identity." Paper delivered at the 1995 Annual Meeting of the American Political Science Association, Chicago, August 31–September 3.

Olsen, Laurie. *Made in America.* New York: New Press, 1997.

Page, Ann L., and Donald A. Clelland. "The Kanawha County Textbook Controversy: A Study of the Politics of Life Style Concern," *Social Forces* 57 (September 1978): 1.

People for the American Way. *Looking at History.* Washington, D.C.: People for the American Way, 1985.

———. *We The People.* Washington, D.C.: People for the American Way, 1987.

Perry, Theresa, and James W. Fraser, eds. *Freedom's Plow*. New York: Routledge, 1993.

Piasecki, Frank. "Norma and Mel Gabler: The Development and Causes of Their Involvement Concerning the Curricular Appropriateness of School Textbook Content." Ph.D. diss., North Texas State University, 1982.

Pinar, William F. "Notes on Understanding Curriculum As a Racial Text." In *Race, Identity, and Representation in Education*, ed. Cameron McCarthy and Warren Crichlow. New York: Routledge, 1993.

Powell, Walter W. *Getting into Print*. Chicago: University of Chicago Press, 1985.

"Rainbow Revised." Editorial in *New York Times*, 30 June 1993, 120.

Ravitch, Diane. "Diversity and Tradition." Letters to the Editor. *New York Times*, 28 February 1990, A26.

———. "Multiculturalism: E Pluribus Plures." In *Race and Ethnic Conflict: Contending View on Prejudice, Discrimination, and Ethnoviolence*, ed. Fred L. Pincus and Howard J. Ehrlich. Boulder, Colo.: Westview, 1994.

Rieder, Jonathan. *Canarsie*. Cambridge, Mass.: Harvard University Press, 1985.

Roberts, Sam. "In Brooklyn's District 15, Divisions of the City Are Reflected in the Campaign." *New York Times*, 2 May 1993, 149.

Rubin, Lillian B. *Families on the Fault Line*. New York: HarperCollins, 1994.

Sack, Kevin. "Cuomo Wary of Revisions in Curriculum." *New York Times*, 16 July 1991, B1,4.

Sadker, Myra, and David Sadker. *Failing at Fairness*. New York: Touchstone, 1994.

Schlafly, Phyllis, ed. *Child Abuse in the Classroom*. Westchester, Ill.: Crossway Books, 1984.

Schlesinger, Jr., Arthur. *The Disuniting of America*. New York: Norton, 1992.

Schomburg, Carl E. "Texas and Social Studies Textbooks." *Social Education* (January): 58–63.

"School Board's Confusing Signals." Editorial in *New York Times*, 12 December 1992, 122.

Scott, W. Richard. "Unpacking Institutional Arguments." In *The New Institutionalism in Organizational Analysis*, ed. Paul DiMaggio and Walter W. Powell, 164–82. Chicago: University of Chicago Press, 1991.

Seidman, Steven. *Contested Knowledge*. Cambridge, Mass.: Blackwell, 1994.

Sidel, Ruth. *Battling Bias: The Struggle for Identity and Community on College Campuses*. New York: Penguin, 1994.

Sleeter, Christine E. "How White Teachers Construct Race." In *Race, Identity, and Representation in Education*, ed. Cameron McCarthy and Warren Crichlow, 157–71. New York: Routledge, 1993.

Sleeter, Christine E., and Peter L. McLaren, eds. *Multicultural Education, Critical Pedagogy, and the Politics of Difference*. New York: SUNY Press, 1995.

Tabor, Mary B. W. "S.I. Drops Gay Issues from Student Guide." *New York Times*, June 1992, B3.

Task Force on Minorities: Equity and Excellence. *A Curriculum of Inclusion*. Albany: New York State Education Department, July 1989.

Tuchman, Gaye. *Edging Women Out*. New Haven, Conn.: Yale University Press, 1989.

————. *Making News*. New York: Free Press, 1978.

Tyack, David, and Elisabeth Hansot. *Managers of Virtue*. New York: Basic, 1982.

Verhovek, Sam Howe. "New York Education Chief Seeks New Stress on Non-white Cultures." *New York Times*, 7 February 1990, A1, 4.

————. "Plan to Emphasize Minority Cultures Ignites a Debate," *New York Times*, 21 June 1991, A1.

————. "Way Cleared for Changes in Curriculum." *New York Times*, 26 July 1991, B1.

Waters, Mary. *Ethnic Options*. Berkeley: University of California Press, 1990.

Weissman, Arnie. "Building the Tower of Babel." *Texas Outlook* (Winter 1981–82): 10–33.

Wexler, Phillip. "Structure, Text, and Subject: A Critical Sociology of School Knowledge." In *Cultural and Economic Reproduction in Education: Essays on Class, Ideology, and the State*, ed. Michael W. Apple, 275–303. London: Routledge & Kegan Paul, 1982.

Williams, Raymond. "Base and Superstructure in Marxist Cultural Theory." In *Rethinking Popular Culture*, ed. Chandra Mukerji and Michael Schudson. Berkeley: University of California Press, 1991.

————. *Marxism and Literature*. Oxford, U.K.: Oxford University Press, 1977.

Wirt, Frederick M., and Michael W. Kirst. *Schools in Conflict*. Berkeley, Calif.: McCutcheon Publishing, 1982.

Wolff, Janet. *The Social Production of Art*. New York: St. Martin's, 1981.

Wong, Kenneth K., and Tom Loveless. "The Politics of Textbook Policy: Proposing a Framework." In *Textbooks in American Society*, ed. Philip G. Altbach, Gail P. Kelly, Hugh G. Petrie, and Lois Weis. Albany, N.Y.: SUNY Press, 1991.

Wong, Sandra L. "School Textbooks: The Social Selection of Educational Knowledge," Ph.D. diss., Yale University, 1990.

Yates, Douglas. *Bureaucratic Democracy*. Cambridge, Mass.: Harvard University Press, 1982.

Young, Michael F. D., ed. *Knowledge and Control*. London: Collier MacMillan, 1971.

Zurcher, Louis A., and R. George Kilpatrick. *Citizens for Decency: Antipornography Crusades as Status Defense*. Austin: University of Texas Press, 1976.

# Index

147

# About the Author

**Sandra Leslie Wong** is assistant professor of sociology at Colorado College. She is the author of several articles on cultural struggles and institutional practices. Her current interests include the construction of racial and ethnic identities and the educational experiences of American minorities.